ETHNIC ETHICS

ETHNIC ETHICS

The Restructuring of Moral Theory

Anthony J. Cortese

State University of New York Press

Published by
State University of New York Press, Albany

© 1990   State University of New York

For information, address the State University of New York Press,
State University Plaza, Albany, NY 12246

Library of Congress Cataloging-in-Publication Data

Cortese, Anthony Joseph Paul.
    Ethnic ethics : the restructuring of moral theory / by Anthony J.
Cortese.
        p.   cm.
    Includes bibliographical references.
    ISBN 0–7914–0279–7. — ISBN 0–7914–0280–0 (pbk.)
    1. Ethics. 2. Ethnicity. 3. Pluralism (Social sciences)
I. Title.
BJ1031.C67   1990
170'.89—dc20   89–39656
                                                                    CIP

10 9 8 7 6 5 4 3 2 1

Con Honor Para Mis Padres,

Rachel y Joseph Cortese

The last shall be first.

—*King James Bible*

If not now, when?

—*Hillel*

The power of reason
and the flowers of deep feelings
seem to serve me
only to deceive me.

—*Joni Mitchell, "Song For Sharon"*

CONTENTS

ACKNOWLEDGMENTS

My special appreciation goes to the late Lawrence Kohlberg; our discussions on cultural differences in morality were helpful in the development of this book. His work has influenced my own—as well as many others—probably more than anyone else. I would like to give thanks to Fabio Dasilva and Joseph W. Scott, who read and provided critical remarks on a previous draft. They, along with Julian Samora, have provided firm guidance since my graduate training; for this, I am very appreciative.

I would also like to acknowledge the following for reading all or part of an earlier draft and furnishing comments: Jeffrey C. Alexander, Robert J. Antonio, William Sims Bainbridge, Carolyn Chantz, Stjepan G. Mestrovic, Scott McNall, Ray Schmitt, Richard Stivers, Edward A. Tiryakian, and T. R. Young. I would like to thank Alissa C. Boehm, Mark J. Murphy, and Jeffrey F. Sype for their typing and spirited support. I thank Norma P. Garcia for her assistance with the references and John Mears for his expertise on 18th century Germany.

Thank you Amber Richelle Cortese.

Introduction

Too much of a good thing is wonderful.

—*Mae West*

Heaven and hell, however, hang together.
—*Max Horkheimer and Theodor Adorno,* Dialectic of Enlightenment

The major goal of this book is to contribute to the advancement of ethical analysis by addressing: (1) several key issues of moral theory that appear to be crucial to the empirical investigation of moral cognition, namely, ethnicity, culture, and language; (2) conceptual problems linked to justice and objectivistic–subjectivist tensions; and (3) methodological approaches to moral judgment. My starting points are the theories of moral development as formulated by Jean Piaget and Lawrence Kohlberg. I have found limitations in their models based on my own research on moral judgment: The literature on moral theory appears to view Anglo-American culture as universal in defining moral development, while unable to recognize virtually all-white research samples as a methodological problem. My central thesis is that morality based on justice cannot be purely subjective, in the sense that it cannot be derived from the principles of individuals alone. Nor can it be purely objective (e.g., universal rules).

Against the individualistic Kohlbergian view I would like to bring the position that morality is socially and culturally constructed, not based on the rational principles of individuals. I borrow from Emile Durkheim the suggestion that ethical conduct is motivated by a person's "attachment to society" (Hall 1987). He interpreted human nature as basically social. We will see in Chapter 2 that Piaget's model of moral development is, in fact, derived from Durkheim's work. Piaget agreed with Durkheim that the ethical reasoning of children is construed partially by pervasive or emerging social conditions, not by the self-driven cognitive capacities of individuals. Morality, consequently, presumes the existence of patterns and rules that transcend the individual. It is only through social relationships that comprehension of, respect for, and adherence to such rules occur. Piaget completely agreed with Durkheim's notion of moral facts as social, associated with the functional and structural development of collective groups. However, Piaget criticized Durkheim for not acknowledging the crucial qualitative shift from constraint to cooperation in the mental structure of individuals.

Although Piaget declared that there is a culturally invariant series of moral stages, I maintain that the number, content, and order of the stages vary across cultures and subcultures. Kohlberg asserts that morality is located in the psychological structures of the individual; by contrast, I conclude that moral reasoning and behavior are determined largely by social factors—role demands, class interests, national policies, and ethnic antagonisms. One cannot be moral in an immoral social role, whatever one's childhood socialization, psychological predispositions, or commitment to abstract principles. Morality is to be found in the structure of society, not in the structure of human cognition. The key to morality is in social relations, not abstract rational principles. Ethnic background, gender, role demands, and socioeconomic status contradict the developmental stage sequence as proposed by Kohlberg.

The notion of a sociology of moral judgment is not new. Durkheim viewed morality as a "social fact"(see Traugott 1978). His use of the concepts *mind* and *social fact* refers to his "realist" position in sociological matters. Given Durkheim's wholism, he posited a trans-individual psychology beyond a simple monadic view of social beings. Certainly, this was a reaction to Jean Gabriel de Tarde, ([1903] 1962) and his collective psychology. But considering the preface to the second edition of Durkheim's *The Rules of Sociological Method* ([1903] 1982), Durkheim clearly disavowed a simplistic conception of a "collective mind." Parallel to his position is Wilhelm Dilthey's (1977, [1957] 1978) approach to "objectifications" of the human mind. Given the concern of Durkheim with an empirical basis for sociology (rather than a reflective sociology), the epistemological foundation always had to refer to a collective product, such as law, which he used methodologically in most of his works (e.g., *The Division of Labor in Society*, [1893] 1933, *Suicide*, [1897] 1951, *Incest*, 1963). Accordingly, the concepts do not refer to an epistemological position, but rather to a methodological one. In any case, for Durkheim, the initial problem was the maintenance of stability in social life. Correspondingly, we find in him (as later in Talcott Parsons

1951, [1949] 1968) an emphasis on the normative character of social life. This classical position should in no way be taken as the only theoretical alternative; consider, for example, the contrasting position of Marx ([1884] 1961, [1857–1858] 1971, [1867–1895] 1967), among others.

I am particularly interested in how ethnic background affects moral reasoning and moral judgment. During the past ten years, I have been listening to Chicano, black, Asian, and white children, adolescents, and adults discuss their views of morality. I have questioned them and, in response, they have defended their positions, expressing views about themselves and their relationship with others. What I heard was not always what I had expected. Kohlberg's theory of moral development appeals to a transcendental level of morality in order to engage in moral discourse. In doing so, his ethical system provides a blanket solution for all moral problems. Kohlberg has attempted to support his theory with empirical evidence; extensive data have been presented to support the theory.

In this book, I attempt to bring up some of the more serious theoretical and methodological problems related to empirical analysis of Kohlberg's theory. I dispute some of the empirical claims; his evidence is not as conclusive as he implies. Aside from empirical problems there are difficulties with the philosophical and epistemological assumptions used to support Kohlberg's framework. In addition to social scientific analysis, his theory needs grounding in moral philosophy. As Kohlberg (1984) has indicated, science can test whether a philosopher's conception of morality phenomenologically fits the psychological facts. But science cannot go on to justify that conception of morality as what morality ought to be. In other words, the empirical verification of a particular theory of morality does not directly confirm the normative validity of Kohlberg's theory of justice as reversibility. Reversibility or "moral musical chairs" applies the Golden Rule; when making a moral judgment one assumes the position of the other in arguing one's claim. In other words, would you consider your choice or action fair if you were in the other person's shoes. Recently, Kohlberg has turned to Jurgen Habermas to support his assumption that morality is justice based on universal rationality.

I address this tension between empirical science and a transcendental level of knowledge, a recurring problem in the social sciences. I offer a counter thesis to Kohlberg's, and posit an alternative explanation of moral judgments by ethnic minorities, based on my own research. I argue that moral issues must be resolved in the context of particular cultural groups. Although many cross-cultural studies have been conducted to test the validity and universal applicability of Kohlberg's theory, how ethnicity affects moral reasoning has not been examined. I provide a critical analysis of ethnicity in relation to moral judgment. Neither Piaget nor Kohlberg ever resolve the dilemma of how a morality of autonomous rationality is to be derived from the traditional teaching or morality, understood as submission to social authority. One of my objectives is to expose the importance of this dilemma in understanding the role of language in moral theory.

Habermas, a student of linguistic analysis, has been particularly interested in the nature of "speech acts." He has used Piaget and Kohlberg's cognitive development approach to morality in order to examine society through acts of communication. Following Kohlberg has allowed Habermas to maintain that "universalistic, critical thought is grounded in the normal development of the human mind" (Alexander 1985: 400). In other words, Habermas has taken from Kohlberg the argument that critical rationality inherently emerges in the course of individual human development. Consequently, the epistemological implications of Kohlberg's model provide the grounding for critical theory. It is no surprise that the issue of moral reasoning has recently become increasingly important and has been hotly debated in European sociology, especially in West Germany. The English translation of recent works by Habermas and Wolfgang Schlucter (1981), who also uses Kohlberg's framework, corroborates the importance of the topic of moral reasoning for social theory to a growing number of American sociologists. The question of moral development and Kohlberg's writings are likely to gain recognition in becoming more pivotal to contemporary sociological theory and the sociology of knowledge.

The present book links Kohlberg's views to sociological theory. It is interdisciplinary, with roots in the sociology of knowledge, moral philosophy, developmental psychology, and race/ethnic relations. I examine social class, gender, and ethnic differences in moral judgment and critique the cognitive-development model. In opposition to Kohlberg, I argue that moral development is culturally and socially determined. Moral judgment reflects the structure of social relations, not the structure of human cognition.

Chapter 1 lays out the cognitive development approach to moral reasoning. I examine the ethical system of Immanuel Kant from which the philosophical assumptions of Piaget and Kohlberg are derived. I also touch on John Rawl's theory of justice, because it is central to Kohlberg's highest stage of moral development. The history of the concept of moral judgment as devised by Piaget, in his pioneering study of moral development in children, is reviewed. I then focus on Kohlberg's elaboration of Piaget's theory, and his continuation of this tradition in moral judgment research. Finally, I examine the sociohistorical context out of which Kohlberg's influential work emerged.

Chapter 2 focuses on the sociohistorical conditions that have shaped knowledge, the study of language, and our conceptions of morality. I examine the philosophical distinction between "object" and "subject," central to my discussion of knowledge, language, and morality. As throughout this book, I consider attempts to solve the object–subject dilemma by Durkheim, Piaget, Kohlberg, and Habermas as they address the development and restructuring of moral theory relative to knowledge and language. Next, I analyze the link between morality and language through Durkheim's concept of language as a social fact, and the etymology of language as salient to the teaching of morality.

In the third chapter I explicate the relationship between moral development and the sociology of knowledge. I trace the sociology of knowledge back to Karl Mannheim, who viewed knowledge as a social product, revealing much about the age in which ideas arose or in which they were dominant. Chapter 3 also characterizes Kohlberg's six stages of moral reasoning. I discuss Kohlberg's specific meaning of justice, and employ his description of stage-specific sociomoral norms in general and the operation of justice in equality, equity, reciprocity, prescriptive role taking, and universality. Thus, in the first three chapters, I have moved from the most abstract philosophical assumptions (Chapter 1) to the middle-range concerns of the social context of language (Chapter 2) to the sociology of knowledge and to Kohlberg's specific and concrete six-stage theory of moral reasoning (Chapter 3).

Chapter 4 examines problems with measuring moral judgment. I devote this entire chapter to methodology because of its implications for theory. The construction of a research instrument and scoring system that validly measure moral judgment in individuals is crucial. If the methodology is unreliable, infering anything substantial about Kohlberg's theory is seriously hampered.

Chapter 5 analyzes the effect of ethnic background and social class on human development. I explain how modes of moral reasoning vary according to cultural backgrounds. I provide a critique of the cognitive development framework, including recent feminist thought, and critically evaluate the data which have been presented to support the cultural universality of moral stages. I then relate cross-cultural studies to the moral styles that I found in my research on ethnic groups.

Chapter 6 works toward a theoretical framework for subcultural differences in moral reasoning. I provide conclusions based on my empirical research and critique of the cognitive development model. I work toward a synthesis of the concepts of personal autonomy, social constraint, stratification, and social emancipation. By establishing the need to examine the subcultural contexts of moral issues, I hope to contribute a new and useful perspective to moral theory.

Chapter 7, the final chapter, uses Durkheim's dualistic conceptualization of language to criticize the directions that moral theory has taken through Kohlberg and Habermas. I draw out some of the conceptual intersections between Habermas and Kohlberg, and highlight problems for Habermas that result from his tendencies to borrow from Kohlberg. The objective–subjective dimension of social reality provides the framework for my discussion of morality and the sociology of knowledge. Morality is problematic because it is in fact both objective and subjective. Although morality is sometimes materialized as a "social fact," it does not always crystallize in an objective form. Thus morality can also be intersubjective, existing only in the consciousness of individuals and between them. Habermas's account of the evolution of normative frameworks of interaction is based on the assumption of a link between subjective personality and objective social development. This is the major thread that weaves, in some form, through the moral theories of Durkheim, Piaget, Kohlberg, and Habermas.

I would like to note at the outset that my argument is not statistical. That is to say, it does not focus on the representativeness of the racial and ethnic groups studied nor on the generalizability of the data to the larger population. My approach, instead, is interpretive, based on the demonstration that the examples presented point to a different approach to conceptualizing morality. Because of the nature of the subject matter, interpretation is necessary to grasp the structure of moral reasoning; total objectification is neither possible nor desirable. Accordingly, this work is bounded by the nature and context of my observations and mirrors my own interpretive framework. Just as all data rely on theory, every observation depends on a particular perspective. All data must be interpreted; I offer an interpretation that is contextually relevant to the subcultures of the populations studied.

1

The Cognitive Development Approach to Morality: Philosophical Assumptions

> Justice is subsumed in law.
> —*Max Horkheimer and Theodor Adorno*, Dialectic of Enlightenment

> Through law you can protect the people that are bad just as much as you can protect the people that are good.
> —*Subject Number 60 (white male now an attorney)*.

In this book, through cultural analysis, I expand Kohlberg's six-stage theory of moral reasoning into the sociological domain. Of particular interest are ethnic differences in moral judgment. In order to anchor the cognitive development approach to morality, we first turn to the ethical system of Kant, from which the philosophical assumptions of Piaget and Kohlberg are derived.

Kant: The Foundation of Moral Judgment

Immanuel Kant views human consciousness as intentional, active, voluntary, and rational (Aiken 1962; Beck 1969; Cassirer 1981; Kant 1963). He also argued that people are sociable, which makes it possible to have generally compatible relations with others. But he also saw humans as competitive and self-sufficient. Accordingly, there is a conflict between what Kant regarded as positive and negative impulses. In short, Kant proposed a clearly divided—if not paradoxical—conception of human nature. This dualistic notion of human consciousness can be viewed as parallel to the broad dialectical relationship between subject and object which has guided the

7

writing of Arthur Schopenhauer, Wilhelm Wundt, Emile Durkheim, Jean Piaget, Lawrence Kohlberg, and Jurgen Habermas.

Kant's philosophical model was developed in reaction to and as a criticism of rationalism and empiricism. On the Continent, philosophers such as Descartes, Spinoza, and Liebnitz had advanced the spread of rationalist thought. Rationalism is the method of establishing principles by reason, or deduction, usually involving premises stating general ideas or principles (Fuller [1938] 1955). Rationalism is opposed to both empiricism and intuition. Pure mathematics is the prime example of rationalism. Empiricism, on the other hand, had been espoused by the British philosophers—Locke, Hume, Berkeley.

According to empiricism, all knowledge must be validated by sense experience; whatever is knowable is known directly by sense data or inferred from propositons based on sense data. Empiricism is opposed to rationalism and to knowledge by intuition (Fuller [1938] 1955). This implies an antagonism toward "innate ideas" as *a priori* structures of the mind and forms of thinking, and toward entities, whether material or immaterial, that transcend experience, and toward the pretension of reason to discover truths outside and apart from sense experience. All factual propositions are *a posteriori.* Reason is thus constrained by perception. The mind, according to Locke, is not a collection of innate ideas but rather a tabula rasa, a blank tablet written upon purely by experience.

Kant was content with neither rationalism nor empiricism; he developed a third major philosophy, that of idealism. Idealism is the theory that reality is of the nature of mind or of idea (Fuller [1938] 1955). Kant recognized the existence of two dimensions of reality, the "starry sky above" and the "moral law within." He used these symbols to acknowledge the presence of both objective and subjective dimensions of reality. The "starry sky above" refers to objective reality, the world of appearances, and as such can be examined scientifically. The moral law within depicts a subjective reality to be pursued by an ethical scheme. Although Kant made a crucial distinction between science and morality, the creative and rational nature of the human mind plays a crucial role in both.

In *Critique of Pure Reason*, Kant ([1781] 1950) differentiated between *noumena*, or things in themselves, and *phenomena*, or things as they appear to an active human mind. Science and other objective knowledge can only deal with the world of appearances or phenomena; it cannot touch ultimate reality, the world of noumena. Kant went beyond the empiricist focus on sensory experience, suggesting that the human mind imposes order on the chaos of appearances. We are not able to comprehend isolated phenomena simply by perceiving them; rather, the mind constructs meaning holistically. We impose relationships between phenomena through reason. Kant argued that humans have the inherent ability to use such universal structures of thought. This basic premise has guided the theories of Piaget, Kohlberg, and Habermas, to be discussed later.

In *Critique of Pure Reason* ([1788] 1949), Kant affirmed that human conduct is based on rationality; it is this capacity that distinguishes us from other animals, which act on pure instinct. Human instinct, however, can be mediated by using categorical ethical imperatives. Kant places a primacy on the value of the individuals: one should treat oneself and others as an end, never as a means. The particular historical period in which Kant lived clearly was important to his beliefs. Kant's emphasis on individual rights is in the spirit of the Enlightenment, which gave personal freedom a preeminent position, in reaction to the dogmatic authority of church and state.

Kant's conceptualization of society parallels his image of human nature's focusing on self-sufficiency and social compatability. The perfect society would spotlight the primacy of individual freedom and private property rights, to be upheld by the state. The state would provide the collective conscience that resolves disputes that may emerge among competitors and the holders of property.

Because of our physicality, we humans face an objective reality subject to the scientific laws of nature. But given the openness of human freedom and desire, we also have a subjective spirit that cannot be captured by positivistic methodology or deterministic systems. Fundamental to Kant is the distinction between laws of nature and normative principles—between *de facto* and *de jure* questions.

Kant would not accept the principle of causality on which science depends. Consequently, for him science is no closer to knowledge than religion. There is no validity to the claim by science that there are invariable laws of nature. The scientist's intellectual system ultimately rests on a faith that has no more rational basis than the beliefs of the priest, the prophet, or the medicine man. Thus, ultimate truth is impossible. Truth only expresses relations between ideas; it tells us nothing about the world of life. A theorem indicates nothing beyond what is implied by the concepts that it embodies.

Kant's focus on the discerning mind would later provide the underpinnings for cognitive development theory. The mind composes the raw material of sensory experience into a symphony of conceptualized phenomena. Kant was not a pure idealist. In opposition to idealism—the theory that reality exists only in the nature of the mind or in the idea—Kant acknowledged the existence of "things in themselves" outside the mind. In fact, his dualistic conceptualization of reality—the independent reality of noumena, reality not known in perceptual experience, and of phenomena, the objects of possible experience (everything that appears under the forms of time and space or other structures of cognition)—is the major thesis of his entire philosophy. Methodological concepts and principles of inquiry are not privy to the nature or essence of things. Rather, they are procedural rules and concepts that are adhered to for practical prediction and control of phenomena or appearances. Kant bitterly opposes all pretensions to positivistic and metaphysical knowledge of reality.

Ethical issues do not aim to describe or predict matters of fact. Instead, they indicate what we should do and how we should live. Practical (i.e., moral) reason does not yield pure knowledge but pragmatic principles designed to assist us in making judgments. Kant suggested that moral reasoning helps to resolve problems of the will which surface from (a) conflicts among desires or predispositions, and (b) conflicts between natural desires or predispositions and our sense of duty. Accordingly, Kant proposed that there are two kinds of imperatives. First, there are hypothetical imperatives that tell what we must do to satisfy desires. For example, if I wish to maintain my health, then I ought to get enough sleep. Second, there are categorical imperatives that tell us what we ought to do; they are unconditional and non-hypothetical. Using hypothetical imperatives, one may act according to one's tendencies. Categorical imperatives, however, require that one obey them regardless of personal inclinations. They impersonally direct us as rational moral beings.

The notion of law is crucial to grasping the Categorical Imperative, with its focus on the validity of its application without exception. Such moral laws indicate what ought to be the case, not necessarily what is the case. The Categorical Imperative specifies that we ought to embrace as our rules of conduct in any pragmatic context only those precepts that we could consistently determine to be universal natural laws. Kant assumes that we have free will to do or not to do what such moral laws prescribe. Our physicality makes us subject to natural laws. In other words, our bodies are phenomena functioning within the dimensions of time and space, and thus subject to the maxims of physics and physiology. In short, *pure* reasoning is based on the intellect and deals with science; *practical* reasoning, conversely, is based on free will and deals with ethics. Ethics can still be rational, but not purely theoretical.

According to Kantian thought, it is not necessary to assume that the category of cause and effect applies beyond spatial and temporal issues. Kant believed that we relate to a moral dimension outside of space and time. The "metaphysical" laws of morality are thus congruous with the laws of scientific methodology. The belief in free will assumes that humans are members of a rational spiritual system. As a feasible obligation, we must believe in a Being or God who alone can secure our immortality and consequently give meaning to moral life. We have no proof for moral "truths," but, as moral agents, we must accept them. Such beliefs are acts of faith that can never be proven or disproven. The gist of morality gives support to moral experience and conduct. But it does not dole out claims about the "created" world. We accept religious tenets on faith alone. Human behavior can typically be seen to be based on two different types of inclinations. We can act from legal necessity or compulsion. But we can also act out of the intrinsic goodness of the action.

Critique of Kant

Kant's universal ethical system is rooted in the sociohistorical conditions of his time. Eighteenth-century Germany was not yet unified; it was divided into numerous small states. (An overview of German political divisions in the eighteenth century can be found in Anderson 1961: 241–248. For a discussion of how this political situation developed, see Holborn 1968, Chapter 1.) Consequently, overall social order and law were problematic. Germany's political development, retarded compared to that of France and England, was paralleled by the immature development of philosophical and moral thought. Given the substantial variation in legal codes and values and related moral stances in Germany at that time, Kant sought to establish a moral framework that was rational, not based on empiricism.

Three concepts are central to Kant's system: freedom, eternity, and God. Kant assumed that the actions of humans were based on free will, ultimately free of causality. This supposition opposes much of sociological theory, which views humans as essentially socially determined. Moreover, humans were not genetically, historically, economically, or otherwise determined. Kant, however, did recognize the power of these forces; the point is that free will allows one to act in spite of these forces. Freedom also implied that one cannot be constrained physically, cognitively, or emotionally when acting as a moral agent. In any situation of domination, moral considerations are distorted. For Kant, obligation implies judgment but not action. That is, one must have the freedom to act; if that is not available, moral duty or obligation is not possible. Since the action is an option, moral action will not necessarily follow. Freedom involves the option of whether to act on obligation.

The notion of eternity was also crucial to Kant's framework. Human reason was universal and eternal, while empirical observation was not. Kant saw the need to construct a moral system that went beyond space and time. Recognizing the disparity of value structures from one cultural setting to another and from one point in time to another, rational consciousness was the only possibility for a universal ethical system.

Finally, the idea of God was essential. Human reason was based on direct perception or on intuition. Faith was necessary if one were to rely on rationality. Kant saw "god" as a social construct encompassing the search for a universal code of justice. The construction of God was necessary to answer the question: Why be moral in the first place? Kant's God should not be confused with theological positions which view morality as transcendental and God as the source for moral commands.

For Kant, a moral act is one on which all unconstrained, rational human beings could agree. He tried to construct a universal morality that was not based on faith in God. Kant defined moral duty as respect for law. Law becomes a command or, in Kant's terms, an "imperative." The source of the imperative is not an authoritative human, for that would only represent the wishes of an individual. Who is to say whether one person's commands are more moral than those of another? For Kant, moral authority rested on reason. He believed that human reason engenders an imperative assumed to be valid for all rational persons. It reflects neither human nor divine will. It contains no hidden agenda. It sails under its true colors. And, finally, it does not have any exclusive justification. Kant's morality is duty merely for the sake of duty itself. Thus, the imperative is categorical. Only behavior that holds to be a universal law, binding on all rational beings, is moral. Such morality has no human authority. It does not claim to offer emancipation for humans from the difficulties of human experience. It does not argue for a better society. Duty is the nature of moral obligation, as distinguished from all obligations that are merely human (i.e., the conventional ethics of customs and laws).

Reason replaces God as moral authority. But there are problems with the creation of duty by reason:

> The idea of a command in the absence of any commander is inherently absurd, as is the idea of obligation or duty which is not a duty to any person or persons. . . . An obligation is inherently an obligation to some person or group, divine or human, and can no more stand by itself, without relationship to any such being, than can, say, the idea of being a descendant, or spouse, or having a debt. (Taylor 1985: 92).

The concept of duty implies that one assumes a role of moral obligation. But for every role there must be a corresponding or complementary role. One cannot be a teacher without students, a leader without followers, a parent without offspring, or an order-giver without an order-taker. A role necessitates a relationship. Duty and obligation require two parties: one who is obligated and another to whom the first person is obligated.

The concept of justice as formulated by Kant may be viewed as an attempt to reconcile objective and subjective morality. Justice, for Piaget, emerges from private rituals through the intervention of public authorities to create social contracts democratically agreed upon with careful regard for due process and utilitarianism. This leads to the contractarianism of John Rawls at the heart of Kohlberg's highest stages of morality. Rawls follows Kant's lead with economic-psychological theories of rational choice by mutually disinterested individuals with equal rights, to achieve universal principles of justice as fairness adjusted to the bureaucracies of the administrative state and a corporate economy. In defining justice as fairness, Rawls and Kohlberg's orientation refers to relations of liberty, equality, reciprocity, and contract between persons.

Rawls: Theory of Justice

Duty, for Rawls and Kohlberg, centers on justice, giving each person his or her due. Justice is the primary and general moral virtue of a society and of an individual. (Both utility and fairness are virtues regulating individual relationships and individual–societal relationships). Accordingly, moral judgments have the central function of resolving interpersonal and social conflicts of rights and duties. Moral judgment implies equilibrium, balancing, or reversibility of claims.

Rawls' (1971) theory of justice gives Kohlberg's framework a philosophic and normative grounding, something that no amount of supportive data alone could directly provide. Kohlberg uses Rawls' theory as a rational model for parts of his Stage 6 of moral development. It is consistent with the equilibration and reversibility that characterizes Piaget's structure of stages. Kohlberg adopts Rawls' claim to have achieved a rational consensus for justice.

Formalism is central to the frameworks of Rawls and Kohlberg. There are formal qualities of moral judgments that can be defined or argued about regardless of whether there is agreement on substantive matters. That is, a moral stance can achieve consensus on the definition of morality without reaching consensus on the contents of moral principles.

Kohlberg uses Rawls' criterion of reversibility as the primary criterion of justice. Reversibility is what makes solutions to moral dilemmas just from the view of all relevant parties. Kohlberg's Stage 6 centers on ideal role taking or "moral musical chairs." Each person imaginatively changes place with every other person in the dilemma until a fair solution emerges. Kohlberg has adopted Rawls' theory of justice in which fairness is the most adequate orientation to problems of justice. He synthesized Rawls' social contract theory with George Mead's (1934) reconstruction of Kant's categorical imperative as universalizable role taking. Ideal role taking makes it possible to argue for a justice based on equity. Thus, one chooses morally from an original position under a "veil of ignornace" about who in the society one is. This results in the support of justice that can be socially agreed upon. A decision reached in that way is in equilibrium since it reflects the stance of all rational persons governed by a conception of justice as ideal role taking. The veil of ignorance requires one to control, not forget, the bias of vested interest when adjudicating moral conflicts. But Kohlberg's Stage 6 is not synonymous with Rawls' position. At Stage 6, one avoids the biasing effect of vested interests by judging their value as legitimate moral claims, not by ignoring them. Role taking requires one to evaluate the various claims and interests in actual situations. Kohlberg's view of moral principles acknowledges the situational context of each moral problem. But moral judgment is reduced to objectification and calculation. Kohlberg's highest stages of morality involves universal principles which are contextually applied but stable, not rendered arbitrary in the face of changing historical circumstance.

Kohlberg agrees with Rawls' stance regarding the formulation of moral principles, the assumption of constructivism. This implies that moral judgments or principles are human constructions generated in social interaction, not innate propositions *a priori* or empirical generalizations of facts in the world. Principles or methods for judging are tentatively applied to moral problems. When there is disparity between principle and intuitive knowledge of moral choice, one reformulates the principle or disregards the moral intuition. Whichever one decides, one moves on to consider other cases, being open to change until one achieves a reflective equilibrium between principles and moral intuition regarding concrete cases.

Moral principles, according to Rawls and Kohlberg, lead to judgments of "deontic" choice. A deontic judgment is a decision concerning what is right. "Deontic judgments typically derive from a rule or principle" (Kohlberg 1984: 517). Kant's categorical imperative results in deontic judgments that answer the question "What act is right to do?." Deontological justice is derived from a prescriptivist conception of moral judgment. Focus is on universalizable or "ought" orientations or morality, not situational ethics. This implies some basic agreement on the conception of morality as justice. A morality of justice involves objective or rational justifications for choice, not subjective reasons for obligation to other people. Personal choices must be objectively defended by conceptions of justice (e.g., contract, trust). This is the objectivist claim, which Kohlberg borrows from Rawls. Accordingly, principles or judgments should be consistently applied to everyone; everybody should accept them if they are to take a moral point of view. There should be universal agreement on the principles of justice which persons of varying particular values and belief systems must share to cooperate. "Respect for tolerance beyond relativism is guaranteed by conceptions of universal rights and fairness" (Kohlberg 1984: 482).

A primary component of Rawlsian constructivism is contractarianism, the notion that moral principles are generated and validated through a consensus among autonomous, rational, and moral persons. Given the veil of ignorance, one makes judgments concerning the basic principles of social justice regardless of one's place in the societal stratification system. The question then becomes: What traditionally recognized principles of emancipation and equity would the free and equal persons themselves agree upon? Kohlberg's Stage 6 relies on Rawls' two principles of justice: liberty and equality. Using the Golden Rule or Rawls' "original position," the Stage 6 thinker plays "moral musical chairs" to decide what is fairest.

Kohlberg's central moral principle is justice, not faith or love. He argues that love involves desirable action, not obligation or duty.

"Choices that are moral obligations are choices not just for ourselves but for all people" (Kohlberg 1984: 484). But, in opposition to Kohlberg, one could argue that faith and love are universal moral obligations, that they are principles on which all persons could agree, that they are a categorical imperative, and that one would love and have faith as one would want all persons to do the same.

Rawls and Kohlberg use a moral methodology to arrive at moral judgment. Moral methodology is prescriptive, impartial, and universal. Moral judgments can be defined regardless of whether there is agreement on substantive matters. The close link between Kantian universalizability and Piagetian reversibility of moral principles have been clearly brought out by Rawls and Kohlberg.

Piaget: Heteronomy and Autonomy

Piaget regarded human development as periods of cumulative joint macro-level development of the mind-body systems built up from experience (Vanderburg 1985). He specialized in the development of moral judgment (Piaget [1932] 1965) and the evolution of intelligence (Piaget 1953; Piaget and Inhelder 1969) in children.

Piaget conceptualized five stages of cognitive development. Children pursue their perception and motor functions in their first two years. Then in the next couple of years language is learned, resulting in symbolic behavior such as make-believe, imitation, role-play, and going beyond the physical here and now. From the age of four to six, answers to questions are approached in an egocentric and relatively superficial way. Children are not yet able to make conversion transferences. (For example, a pint of water in a tall narrow vial will "appear" to be more than that same pint when poured into a short but wide container.) From eight to eleven years, children begin to comprehend and apply logic, some mathematics, classification operations, and the concepts of time and space. Among eleven-to fourteen-year-olds, reasoning advances beyond concrete situations. Children acquire the ability to test hypotheses, construct theories, and make inferences. A child's logical and moral development comes from basic activities during the course of normal development. Structures of cognition emerge from the context of experience.

According to Piaget (1952, 1954), cognitive development is a sequence of universal and invariant stages. Social transmission (e.g., culture, family) was viewed as a primary variable in the rate of development, according to Piaget's early writing (Cortese 1985; Cortese and Mestrovic 1989). Piaget suggested that intellectual development in individuals was largely the consequence of social factors, such as language (Piaget 1926) and parental and peer support and constraint (Piaget [1932] 1965). But while the content of development was socially determined, the structure was not.

The formalism of Kant attributed cognitive value to the abstract structure of verbal judgments and the rational forms of time, space, and causality, regardless of particular concrete content. Piaget, exhibiting the strong influence of Kant, sought to identify the basic logical structures or stages underlying the judgment of children. He indicated how such structures develop and are transformed by outlining the general assumptions of cognitive development theory:

1. Stages imply distinct or qualitative differences in children's modes of thinking and of solving the same problem at different stages.
2. These different modes of thought form an invariant sequence in individual development. While cultural factors may speed up, slow down, or stop development, they do not change its sequence.
3. Each of these different and sequential modes of thought forms a "structured whole." A given stage-response on a task does not just represent a specific response determined by knowledge and familiarity with that task or tasks similar to it; rather it represents an underlying thought-organization [see Cortese 1989a].
4. Cognitive stages are hierarchical organizations. Stages form an order of increasingly differentiated and intergrated structures to fulfill a common fashion. (Piaget 1960: 13–15)

This stage concept became the basis for Kohlberg's school of moral development.

Kantian ethics focuses on respect for human beings. Recall that according to the categorical imperative, persons are to be treated as ends in themselves, not as a means toward another end. In short, Kant viewed morality in terms of justice. Piaget also conceptualized morality as justice but distinguished between a "heteronomous morality of absolute obedience to rules and adult authority and . . . a . . . morality of autonomous mutual respect between equals and of respect for rules as the result of social contract, agreement, and cooperation among equals"(Kohlberg 1984: 225). These two orientations represent two basic levels of moral development— heteronomy and autonomy (Piaget, [1932] 1965). Unilateral respect for parents or other authorities and the rules they prescribe is characteristic of heteronomous morality (morality shaped by others). Mutual respect for peers or equals and a rational respect for rules that guide interaction are characteristic of autonomous morality. It is the nature of social relations and, eventually, societal complexity which structures the type of moral reasoning found in individuals. Morality is more social than psychological, according to Piaget's early works. Later, however, he altered his position, negating the significance of social factors but emphasizing individually generated play and action as the basis for cognition (Piaget 1952, [1955] 1966).

Piaget's ([1932] 1965) emphasis on structure is evident in his study of moral development. He coined the term *moral judgment* and generated moral stages from behavior patterns that he observed in children. Piaget's method was to play marbles with children in Geneva. In response to his questions (e.g., "Who makes the rules?", "Can you change the rules?"), the children explained the rules as they played. Piaget concluded that younger children were solely objective in their moral judgments; that is, they judged an act to be right or wrong solely in terms of the relation of the act to the rule. Older children, however added the subjective to their moral judgments; that is, they took the intentions of a person into account when judging the moral rightness or wrongness of his/her act.

Piaget created methods for identifying stages of moral judgment in children. He observed children playing marbles and focused on their conceptualization and application of rules. Through clinical interviews, Piaget also presented hypothetical moral dilemmas in order to stimulate fresh reasoning in children (Cortese 1986a). The findings of Piaget's research were important, not only for fascinating data, but also as an impetus for other researchers' empirical studies of moral judgment.

Before Piaget's pioneering study of moral judgment ([1932] 1965), children were merely viewed as "incomplete" adults. In other words, they thought like adults, but simply knew less. Piaget, however, found qualitative differences between children's thinking and that of adults. Children applied a coherent but different cognitive structure in order to make sense out of their world. Not only was children's thought different than that of adults but it underwent an irreversible sequence of qualitative transformations as it became adult. The idea that thinking is developmental was, at that time, revolutionary. Piaget also specified dimensions (e.g., moral realism, communicable responsibility, immanent justice, distributive justice, retributive vs. restitutive punishment) in moral judgment. The theory assumes that disparities between people in the manner in which they construct and solve moral problems are determined largely by their concepts of fairness. Piaget created the framework for what would later become "the most extensively used paradigm in cognitive developmental research" (Rest 1979a: 6).

Kohlberg—Extending the Tradition

Kohlberg continued Piaget's ([1932] 1965) work on the development of moral judgment in children. Kohlberg's original study (1958) did not, however, provide evidence to confirm the two-stage theory of Piaget. Recall that Piaget had stated that individuals moved from a stage of heteronomy to one of autonomy. Kohlberg postulated six stages of moral reasoning, but also integrated the heteronomy and autonomy of Piaget's model (Kohlberg 1984). They represented the distinction made between two substages (A and B) at each of Kohlberg's six stages. Nevertheless, these substages have since been removed from the theoretical model and scoring manual (Dawn Schrader, personal communication, October 5, 1987).

Kohlberg's (1984) six moral stages are divided into three major levels: preconventional (Stages 1 and 2), conventional (Stages 3 and 4), and postconventional (Stages 5 and 6).

Preconventional morality is the level of most children under 9, some adolescents, and many adolescent and criminal offenders. Conventional morality is the level of most adolescents and adults in our society and in other societies. Postconventional morality is attained by only a minority of adults and is usually reached only after the age of 20. The term "conventional" refers to conforming to and upholding the rules, expectations, and conventions of society solely on the basis that they are, in fact, society's rules, expectations, or conventions. The individual at the preconventional level of morality has not yet come to really understand and uphold conventional or societal rules and expectations. The individual at the postconventional level of morality understands and generally accepts society's rules and expectations, but acceptance of such rules and expectations is based on formulating and accepting the general moral principles that underlie these rules and expectations (e.g., the right to life, the right to property, upholding social contracts). If these moral principles happen to conflict with society's rules and expectations, the postconventional individual adheres to the principle rather than convention.

At each of the three levels of morality, the relationship between the *self* and *society's rules and expectations* is different (Kohlberg 1984).

At the preconventional level, rules and expectations are external to the self. At the conventional level, the self is identified with or has internalized the rules and expectations of others, especially those of authorities. At the postconventional level, the individual has differentiated his or her self from the rules and expectations of others and defines his or her values in terms of self-chosen ethical principles.

Two features of Piaget's approach have become standard in Kohlberg's structural view of moral development (Edwards 1981: 503). These include: (1) a method, the flexible clinical interview, which allows the tester considerable freedom to probe the "whys" of the subject's belief to uncover the underlying structure; and (2) a theory about causal transition from one stage to the next, that social experience stimulates development by encouraging processes of role taking (the coordination of perspectives of self and others as a basis for choosing).

Kohlberg's last major work (1984) provided a reformulation of the theory. The current formulation represents a substantial amount of revision and expansion (Cortese, 1986b). The domain of moral reasoning was opened up to include "soft stage" development, vis-à-vis "hard stages" of justice. Attention was given to the relationship between moral judgment and moral action. The "care and responsibility" approach to morality (Gilligan 1982) also received careful study. Kohlberg no longer claimed to have empirical or philosophical support for Stage 6, which he claims to be the most desirable and adequate stage of justice reasoning (i.e., most amenable to the criterion of reversibility). He noted that empirical evidence could weaken the normative, theoretical claims, but could not positively "prove" them. Some of Kohlberg's critics (Gibbs. 1979; Habermas 1979; Gilligan 1982) accepted the assumptions of cognitive development theory already mentioned, but criticized his stage definitions, especially at the postconventional level (i.e., Stages 5 and 6). Kohlberg, thus, proposed that the assumptions of cognitive development theory had not been challenged by critics. Kohlberg (1984: 319) stated that

> objectivity is a "moment" of scientific inquiry; that the essence of "truth" value of objectivity does not reside in some reified, permanent, or factual quality inherent in the object of inquiry, but is rather to be found in and understood as a process of understanding, which is the changing relationship between the investigator and what he or she observes.

Data from U.S. subjects (Kohlberg 1963, 1969, 1973; Turiel 1966, 1969; Rest, Turiel, and Kohlberg 1969; Turiel and Rothman 1972; Kuhn 1976) support the claim that individuals develop through these stages in a sequential manner. In cross-cultural studies in Turkey (Turiel, Edwards, and Kohlberg 1978; Nisan and Kohlberg 1982), Israel (Kohlberg, Snarey, and Reimer 1984), British Honduras (Gorsuch and Barnes 1973), India (Parikh 1974), Mexico (Kohlberg 1969), Thailand (Batt 1974), Taiwan (Kohlberg 1969), England (Simpson and Graham 1971), Canada (Sullivan 1975), Kenya (Edwards 1975), New Zealand (Moir 1974), and the Bahamas (White 1974), the same sequence of stages is evident.

Kohlberg, like his predecessor Piaget, assumed that children actively construct social reality. This is in opposition to the social learning paradigm in which children's ideas of morality are merely imitations of adult conceptions of justice. Kohlberg attempted to go beyond internalization models that stressed imitation, cultural relativity, and the teaching of value content. He reintroduced social evolution (Spencer 1899; Hobhouse 1906; Dewey and Tufts 1908), which had been undermined earlier in anthropology and replaced with cultural relativism. According to Kohlberg, structures of moral thought range from simple to complex. Kohlberg had been drawn to the premises of structuralism, before reading Piaget, while "doing diagnostic and research work examining unconscious and affective structures from a psychoanalytic framework" (Kohlberg 1979: vii). For Kohlberg, however, psychoanalysis was inadequate for distinguishing between unconscious mental structures and culturally conforming responses. There were serious problems of interpretation; psychoanalysis could even create the problems that it was designed to cure. The Piaget approach, however, offered great promise; mental structures seemed to be revealed directly.

Kohlberg also turned to McDougall (1908), Dewey ([1895] 1964), Mead (1934), and especially Baldwin (1906) for theoretical guidance (Cortese 1986b). Although his dissertation director, Helen Koch, was not particularly interested in moral development, she proved to be a strong mentor. At the University of Chicago, Kohlberg was influenced by Charles Morris, a philosopher, and Anselm Strauss (Kohlberg, personal correspondence, June 28, 1983). Strauss, a sociologist, was perhaps the first American scholar to work toward a theoretical integration of the cognitive structuralism of Piaget and the symbolic interactionism of Mead (Kohlberg 1984). Kohlberg's approach integrated the cognitivism and formalism of Piaget and the reflexivity of Mead. Krebs (1967), Kramer (1986), Blatt (1969), and

Rest (1969) at Chicago, and Turiel (1965) at Yale, also conducted their dissertation research in moral development.

The Sociohistorical Context

Kohlberg's early work (from 1958 through the early 1960s) received little attention from the scientific community. He was initially regarded as an "odd duck" within American psychology (Brown and Herrnstein, 1975). At that time morality appeared to be a weapon for controlling sex and, possibly, swearing. There was no room for studying moral reasoning through behavioralism, psychoanalysis, or cultural anthropology. The theoretical developments and research generated by Kohlberg can best be appreciated in recognition of the isolation and opposition which he faced.

Tiryakian (1979: 217) indicates that a school in its formative years "may be looked down upon by the larger scientific community, ignored or repudiated for being nonscientific" (which may amount to no more than deviating from "normal" science). Many academicians held the study of cognition in contempt. American psychology in the 1950s and 1960s was dominated by behaviorism, ranging from radical behaviorism to social learning theory, in contrast to Kohlberg's stated view that patterns of behavior are developmental and that reasoning has an underlying structure of stages.

Although not radical by today's standards, at the time "the possibility of examining cognition was hotly debated, as was the notion that there were developmental trends in human behavior" (Rest 1979a: 7). The political arena at the time also helped to suppress the significance of Kohlberg's research. In the Eisenhower era, morality was associated with "stodgy moralists, muddleheaded do-gooders, and Communist-hunters" (Rest 1979a: 3). Yet Kohlberg continued his structural examination of morality.

Kohlberg and Turiel replicated Kohlberg's dissertation research in other cultures: Turkey, Taiwan, and Yucatan. Turiel (1966) published an article based on his dissertation, which tested the stage-order hypothesis. He assessed the moral judgments of adolescents and found that those exposed to the adjacent higher stage would assimilate judgments more than would subjects exposed to stages two above or one below their own. Since then, evidence has suggested that judgments slightly higher than one's own produces optimal assimilation (Berkowitz, Gibbs, and Broughton 1980). For example, a person pretested at Stage 3/4 is exposed to Stage 4 and assimilates to Stage 4.

In Kohlberg's (1958) dissertation, moral stages were viewed, not as true stages, but as Weberian ideal-types (Kohlberg 1979). Since Kohlberg and Turiel used data based on group means, their research did not validate the theory. Rest's (1969) dissertation provided the first evidence for the hierarchical integration of stages.

By the mid-1960s the study of cognition had become a major interest in psychology. This interest paralleled a growing societal concern for moral issues. Kohlberg's theory began to provide answers for a contemporary psychology in crisis and for a conflict-ridden society that demanded ethical progress.

Kohlberg (1969) published "Stage and Sequence: The Cognitive-Developmental Approach to Socialization." This lengthy chapter includes supportive data from the cross-cultural studies and the research of Rest. This optimistic statement provided the school with a proclamation, a new mode of interpreting social reality.

> In 1969, . . . Kohlberg's Center for Moral Development at Harvard was just the place to entertain audacious grand schemes. The Center was filled with energetic activity; there was a sense of being in the vanguard of a new psychological and educational movement. . . . Behaviorism was losing its hold on the field of personality and social development. . . . Soon much interest . . . would be directed towards the processes and organization of thinking. . . . Kohlberg had disregarded Behaviorism's edicts and had a wealth of ideas for extending Piaget's . . . approach. . . . The apathy of psychologists toward the study of morality was changing. The Civil Rights Movement, the student protests, and the debate over the Vietnam War dramatized how differently people think about the issues of social justice. Psychological studies of moral thinking seemed more and more important and relevant. (Rest 1979a: xvii–xviii)

Kohlberg's school now had social relevance and a salvational message. Nevertheless, individual longitudinal data were still needed to validate the invariant sequence of stage structure. Moreover, methodologically, the reliability of the instrument had yet to be established. But the spirit of the manifesto was one of confident, steady advance of the cognitive development paradigm. The six moral stages were posited to form an order of increasing cognitive adequacy (Kohlberg 1971a). They would later be described as different kinds of social perspectives (Kohlberg 1976).

Conclusion

The cognitive development approach to morality can be traced back to the philosophical assumptions of Kant who viewed the human mind as rational, reflective, and intentional. His focus on objective justice heavily influenced the writings of Piaget and Kohlberg. Durkheim, who approached the study of morality empirically, rather than reflectively, made an important impression on Piaget, but not Kohlberg. In particular, Durkheim and Freud saw the need for restraining the subjective elements of human nature in order for humans to be fully moral. Piaget recognized this and acknowledges Durkheim for the salient point that morality may be understood in terms of social constraints. Yet Piaget was never able to shake the Kantian notion that only *unconstrained* consciousness resulted in moral principles and action. This is the focus of the next chapter.

2

The Social Context of Language
and Morality

The great trouble we have in understanding each other, and the
fact that we even lie to each other without wishing to: It is because
we all use the same words without giving them the same meaning.
—*Emile Durkheim*, The Elementary Forms of Religious Life

There's a sign on the wall, but she wants to be sure cause you
know sometimes words have two meanings.
—*Led Zeppelin, "Stairway to Heaven"*

In the Introduction, I have proposed that morality must be understood within a particular cultural and sociohistorical context. I take
issue with the cognitive development framework of morality. Kantian formalism and rationalism, upon which Piaget and Kohlberg's
theories rest, are not able to handle issues of non-uniformity with
their uniform ethical laws. Justice cannot always be attained with
categorical and universal rules. The basic problem with the moral
theories of Kant, Piaget, and Kohlberg is that trying to establish
universal principles of ethics is a futile attempt to conceptualize morality in an objective manner at the expense of subjective reality.

In this chapter, I propose that such subjective dimensions are
crucial to understanding morality. First, I discuss the philosophical
distinction between object and subject. Borrowing from Schopenhauer, Simmel, Wundt, and Durkheim, I suggest that subjective passions and desires are at least as important as objective reason in
understanding morality. Durkheim believed that the etymology of
language is crucial to the teaching of morality. This chapter analyzes
the relationship between morality and language in the context of
what has come to be known as the object–subject debate (Cortese

25

and Mestrovic 1989). This book evaluates attempts to resolve the object–subject dilemma by Durkheim, Piaget, Kohlberg, and Habermas as their theories pertain to the development and restructuring of moral theory relative to language. Durkheim's dualistic conception of language (the private and the collective) parallels the epistemological distinction between subject and object.

The Object–Subject Distinction

The epistemological distinction between object and subject usually begins with the opposition between reality or material "stuff" and our idea or representation of that reality (Lalande [1926] 1980). But ideas and representations imply as much reality as material "stuff" does (e.g., Durkheim's notion of the social fact). Thus, even subjective ideas may be objectively real. Fodor (1981) indicates that empiricism on the objective side of this dualism cannot assert that what is in the mind must first be present in the senses. Reality can only be known as phenomena through ideas and "representations," never directly as Kant's *noumena* or thing-in-itself. This is the gist of Kant's devastating critique of empiricism. Both moral theory and the study of language are affected by the degree of emphasis placed on one or the other side of the object–subject distinction.

Furthermore, what has come to be known as cultural relativism is frequently linked to the object–subject distinction. If objective reality can be apprehended only through the filter of one's subjective perceptions, then it seems to follow that the notion of true knowledge must be surrendered. Accordingly, the truth of moral reality as well as the truth of whatever is communicated through language become suspect. Bloom (1987) stated that the contemporary version of cultural relativism is actually a bastardization of Nietzsche's philosophy, leading to a kind of "immorality" in modern life because all norms are seen as relative and, therefore, non-constraining. While Bloom's thesis is appealing, he does not spell out how or why this bastardization occurred, nor why Nietzsche's philosophy is central. Nevertheless, recent works in the philosophy of the social sciences (e.g., Flew 1985; Trigg 1985) cite the key status of language in beginning to resolve some of these controversies. I shall summarize their arguments briefly in order to set up the logic of my own attempt.

Trigg (1985) and Flew (1985) analyze both sides of the object–subject debate, but refuse to cede the idea of an objective truth to cultural relativism. For example, Trigg maintains that chemistry and physics should not hold "diplomatic immunity" from the charges typically thrown at the social sciences (e.g., being subjective, value-laden, and culture-specific). Is not the pursuit of truth, even in physics, itself a value? What is quantum mechanics about except unobservable entities? Pure observation is not possible, even in chemistry and physics. "The recognition of a substance as 'rock salt,' let alone its classification as a 'sodium salt,' is in no sense a 'raw' experience, uncomplicated by interpretation" (Trigg 1985: 8). In short, there can be no pure facts in any science. Even the "most innocent and detached of observer's reports really involves the application of an elaborate theory" (Flew 1985: 177). Both writers insist that tables, chairs, protons, electrons, and social facts are equally problematic and cannot exist as facts apart from theory and interpretation. Although this seems to be an obvious point epistemologically, Flew is accurate in maintaining that textbooks still depict the social sciences as if they were "developing countries" in relation to the allegedly superior "hard sciences."

If facts need theory and language to "exist", and if theories and language are culturally bound, then is science just a "complex social activity"? What about truth? The cultural relativist position that all objective claims can have validity only against a particular social background is self-defeating: "it destroys itself, since it can no longer claim the kind of truth it needs if others are to take notice of it" (Trigg 1985: 41). If it is true that nothing is really "true" because everything is culturally relative, then even that claim is paradoxically untrue, because it is culturally relative. "The objectively true becomes synonymous with the scientifically accessible" (Trigg 1985: 47). The extreme relativist position is the "rape of reason" because it reduces knowledge to personal taste and opinion, and academic knowledge to bourgeois ideology (Flew 1985). Yet if facts cannot exist apart from theories, how can one believe in objective truth? That is, how can one be a cultural relativist to the extent that one grants that truth is not absolute or independent of theory, yet give reason and truth their traditional dignity without succumbing to dogmatism? This is a dilemma that is pertinent to epistemological as well as moral issues in sociology.

The manner in which Trigg (1985) and Flew (1985) depict this dilemma is noteworthy. They hint at a solution without developing it, one that I shall pursue:

> All the basic notions of logic are and cannot but be involved from the beginning in any learning of a language. . . . [If there are] dif-

ferent conceptions of rationality, then the common element which makes them all conceptions of rationality must be or include whatever is essential for learning any language, and hence for determining what anyone is saying about anything. (Flew 1985: 174)

Trigg's words (1985: 188) are just as weighty:

The understanding of language seems to provide the key to the social sciences. Indeed the mere possibility of learning a language seems hard to explain. Language apparently determines both social and physical reality, rather than reality determining language.

I shall follow this lead and link it to moral theory. Drawing on Saussure, Wittgenstein, and others who have contributed to the philosophical tradition in the study of language, one can conclude the following: Language is partly physical and partly social, partly objective and partly subjective, relative to society yet permanent across generations. As such, it is ideal for analyzing the dualisms and tensions in the object–subject debate as well as debates on moral theory that concern subjective versus objective dimensions of morality. In linguistics, Meillet, Wundt, Durkheim, Saussure, and other turn-of-the-century intellectuals were advancing the study of language beyond Kantianism when they proposed that language ought to be studied as an *idea* (the French *representation* and the German *Vorstellung*) that is no less real than material "stuff."

First one must challenge some aspects of current thinking about the origins of the social sciences. These origins are depicted in Kantian, positivistic, post-Enlightenment terms. Such terms pertain to the objective side of the object–subject distinction. Simmel ([1907] 1987) clearly links the anti-positivistic philosophies of Schopenhauer and Nietzsche to the origins of the social sciences. Schopenhauer's philosophic antagonism between the "will" and the "idea" can be understood as still another refraction of the object–subject distinction, but with an important difference (see Baillot 1927, Ellenberger 1970, Janik and Toulmin 1973, Hamlyn 1980, Magee 1983). Schopenhauer treats will, which stands for "subjective" passion and desire, as a force superior to seemingly more "objective" reason. Freud's "id," Simmel's "life," Nietzsche's "will to power," James' "will to believe," and several other variations of a "will" found in turn-of-the-century writings may be considered as refractions of Schopenhauer's "will." Moreover, one may link Durkheim's opposition between "representations" and the "bottomless abyss" of human desires to Schopenhauer's distinction between the "idea" and the intemperate "will," even though Durkheim has been understood primarily in a postivistic context.

Schopenhauer had challenged the primacy of Kantian rationalism:

> Kant distinguished the world of phenomena and the world of the thing itself, which is inaccessible to our knowledge. Schopenhauer called the phenomena *representations*, and the thing in itself, *will*, equating the will with the unconscious as conceived by some of the romantics; Schopenhauer's will had the dynamic character of blind, driving forces, which not only reigned over the universe, but also conducted man [and woman]. Thus, man is an irrational being guided by internal forces, which are unknown to him and of which he is scarely aware. (Ellenberger 1970: 208)

To be sure, the implication of this is that Schopenhauer reversed the Enlightenment view of human nature in which reason dominates the passions. For Schopenhauer, the "heart" is stronger than the mind, a view that is echoed more in Durkheim and Freud, for example, than in Kohlberg and Piaget. The point is that all of the writers and debates mentioned thus far are modifications of the object–subject distinction, which I wish to connect with moral theory and its relationship to language.

The Language-Morality Bond

Durkheim developed Cartesian and theological concerns with morality into a concern for the "science of moral facts" (Levy-Bruhl 1899). He was interested in social facts in order to create a new science of morality:

> We shall therefore call it "Science of Morality" or "Science of Moral Facts," understanding thereby that it deals with moral phenomena or moral reality as it can be observed either in the present or in the past, just as physics or physiology deals with the facts that they study. (Traugott 1978: 202)

Logue (1983) examines Durkheim's concern with the science of morality within the broad philosophical context of his time, which resonated with the similar ideas of his distinguished colleagues, among them Wundt, Renouvier, Espinas, Guyau, and Bouglé. Their concern with "scientific morality" focused on the concept of justice in the context of the liberal tradition in philosophy, not the conservative focus on social order (Logue 1983). "Justice" served as a rallying cry for socialism as well as one of the major principles of the Third Republic of France. This use of the word *justice* implied a reconciliation between objectivism and subjectivism. "Justice" was an objective social fact, especially for Durkheim, as well as leading to a subjective state of happiness or at least contentment. Modern linguistics began at about the same time that Durkheim started to study morality using the scientific method, there is an important connection between the two which I would like to develop.

Marcel Mauss captured the essence of Durkheim's complex understanding of language with the claim that language is a "total social fact." By "total" Mauss ([1950] 1979: 20) implied that the social fact is simultaneously social, psychological, and physiological. The social dimension relates to the collective meanings of words; the psychological deals with speech and the private use of language; and the physiological refers to the larynx, brain, and other physical organs necessary for speech. Mauss, no less complicated than Durkheim, claims that this move assumed a *homo duplex* within the *homo duplex*. *Homo duplex* refers to the dualism of human nature. Humans are both social and individual. Man's social nature is further divided into material and non-material (e.g., collective representations) aspects. Thus, we have a *homo duplex* within a *homo duplex*. Man's individual nature is also divided: the mind and the body (another *homo duplex* within a *homo duplex*). Language, similarly, forms a *homo duplex* within a *homo duplex*. That is, object and subject are two opposing aspects of a dualism, but the subject is further subdivided into a *homo duplex*, psychological representations versus "the body" (Mauss [1950] 1979: 20–24). This characterization of language parallels Saussure's well-known distinction between *langue* and *parole*, which became the basis of the modern science of linguistics. Saussure ([1916] 1959: 6) asserted that "language [*langue*] is a social fact," assuming at least a part of Durkheim's complicated epistemology.

Doroszewski (1932) and Meillet (1982) wrote that Saussure reproduced Durkheim's notion of the "social fact" in his linguistics. But contemporary sociologists as well as linguists have expressed little interest in the implication of Saussure's claim that language is a social fact. Doroszewski (1932) compared and contrasted Durkheim's ([1895] 1982, [1924] 1974) treatment of social fact with Saussure's ([1916] 1959) treatment of language (see Vendryes 1921, Godel 1969, Gernet 1981). Doroszewski (1932: 91) believed that Saussure's distinction between *langue* and *parole* attempts a reconciliation of the debate between Durkheim and Tarde. The seemingly more collective, "objective" *langue* is a concession to Durkheim, while the more individual, "subjective" *parole* is a concession to Tarde. Doroszewski's view is supported by Mauro ([1967] 1978: 382) and Mounin (1975: 50), though it is virtually ignored in contemporary sociological theory.

There are mutual influences on Saussure and Wilhelm Wundt that cannot be ignored. For example, Wundt—widely esteemed as the father of modern psychology in Germany—foreshadowed both Durkheim and Saussure with his extensive treatment of language (1907) as an integral part of his *Volkerpsychologie*. Durkheim studied under Wundt from 1885 to 1886, and readily admitted Wundt's influence (see Durkheim [1885] 1978: 102; [1887] 1976: 304). In fact, Mauss ([1950] 1979: 12) refers to Durkheim as Wundt's pupil. Durkheim and Fauconnet ([1903] 1982: 208) referred to Wundt's *Volkerpsychologie* as "a study whose subject matter is definite: it aims to investigate the *laws* of collective thought through its objective manisfestations, in particular mythology and language" (emphasis in original). The idea that thought exists in a primitive state of flux— that it is Schopenhauer's indefinite "will" that "objectifies" itself through language—is essential to understanding Durkheim's and other turn-of-the-century conceptions of language.

Wundt has already been linked to Schopenhauer's philosophy (see Ellenberger 1970), which Thomas Mann ([1939] 1955) regards as the foundation of modern psychology. Consider, for example, the following passage from Schopenhauer's *The World as Will and Idea* ([1818] 1977: 238) in the light of the preceding discussion:

> Words and speech are thus the indispensable means of distinct thought. But as every means, every machine, at once burdens and hinders, so also does language; for it forces the fluid and modifiable thoughts, with their infinitely fine distinctions of difference, into certain rigid, permanent forms, and thus in fixing also fetters them.

Durkheim's description of the violence that language commits against thought, even his focus on "constraint" (a word whose etymological roots, the Latin *constringere* and French *entrave*, can be traced to the meaning that something is chained and fettered), seems to be a reflection of Schopenhauer's passage above.

The idea that the subjective dimension of human nature must be constrained, regulated, and controlled for morality, as well as for communication through language to be possible, is central to a host of theories by turn-of-the-century thinkers, especially Freud and Durkheim (see Ellenberger 1970). But so is the converse notion that this subjective element is natural, extemporaneous and therefore beneficial. Consider, for example, Simmel's ([1907] 1987) use of the concept of "life" as a refraction of Schopenhauer's "will to life," as well as the works of Guyay ([1887] 1962) and Toennies' ([1887] 1963) opposition between the "rational will" of *Gessellschaft* versus the "natural will" of *Gemeinschaft*. Durkheim specifically noted Schopenhauer's impact on Toennies' (Traugott 1978: 115). Durkheim agreed with Toennies' description, but would not accept that the "rational will" of *Gessellschaft* was "unnatural." Simmel ([1907] 1987: 105) summarized this tension well:

> Schopenhauer's disposition toward and his explanations of good and evil in the world can all be reduced to one basic thought: Metaphysical will as it is perceived in its absolute unity, before it is splintered by human intellect into a specific individual form, is clearly the potentiality of all pain and misfortune, but it is not the realization of evil. The reality of evil is only given through the process of establishing some spurious goals by the individual, by the struggle of individual forms against one another.

The subjective will, in itself, is beyond good and evil, to cite Nietzsche. Turn-of-the-century intellectuals were struggling with the problem of how the constraints on egoism, which are central to morality, were to be reconciled with the spontaneous and free development of individualism, which was seemingly inevitable. This unresolved tension is as evident in Saussure's opposition between the "objective" *langue* and the "subjective" *parole* as it is in subsequent developments in moral theory.

Durkheim ([1925] 1961, [1938] 1977) pointed out that the etymology of language is crucial to the teaching of morality. As Durkheim ([1938] 1977: 347) indicated, "stylistic training should be understood, first and foremost, not as a means of teaching children to write elegantly and eloquently, but as a more complex exercise in analysis and logical synthesis." For Durkheim, logic and reason are impersonal and, therefore, collective processes related to the development of moral individualism and justice (see Durkheim [1925] 1961: 1–20 *passim*).

Durkheim barely developed these important linkages, but they are intriguing. For example, in *Moral Education*, he writes:

> Rationalism is only one of the aspects of individualism: it is the intellectual aspect of it. We are not dealing here with two different states of mind; each is the converse of the other. . . . Since every advance that it [rationalism] makes results in a higher conception, a more delicate sense of the dignity of man, individualism cannot be developed without making apparent to us as contrary to human dignity, as unjust, social relations that at one time did not seem unjust at all. Conversely, as a matter of fact, rationalistic faith reacts on individualistic sentiment and stimulates it. For injustice is unreasonable and absurd, and, consequently, we are more sensitive to it as we are more sensitive to the rights of reason. Consequently, a given advance in moral education in the direction of greater rationality cannot occur without also bringing to light new moral tendencies, without a greater thirst for justice. ([1925] 1961: 12)

Furthermore, for Durkheim, the rationalistic rules involved in learning language are directly related to the development of morality based upon justice.

I would like to turn to Durkheim's thoughts on language, morality, and justice to establish a context in which the conceptual frameworks of Piaget, Kohlberg, and Habermas may be evaluated. By establishing Durkheim's relationship to the object–subject distinction, and then tracing the relationship of the other key moral theorists to Durkheim's problematic yet productive position, I hope to contribute a new and useful perspective on this discussion. The key point is that all of the moral theorists examined here debated the problem of how various aspects of the "subjective" (private speech, egoism, ideas, individual representations, desires, individualism) may be reconciled with various aspects of the "objective" (the collective meanings of words, collective representations, "reality," society). Often the implicit boundary between object and subject is crossed and their distinctions reversed by these moral theorists. Thus, Durkheim treats collective representations as both objective reality exterior to and constraining individuals as well as subjective meanings that are internalized and individualized.

Piaget was concerned with subjective morality that challenges authoritarian, traditional rules, yet is still somehow objective in that it can be distinguished from egoism. Kohlberg tried to separate the subjective elaboration of conventional norms inherent in post-conventional morality from the equally subjective yet fundamentally different reasoning involved in preconventional morality. Habermas's "speech acts" are similarly private yet intersubjective at the same time that they are meant to represent a morality "higher" than egoism. In other words, all of these thinkers attempt to distinguish narcissism from certain kinds of individualism, that Giddens (1986) has called "moral individualism." Yet critics have argued that this distinction is not readily apparent. For example, Wallach and Wallach (1983) have accused Kohlberg of sanctioning selfishness. The moral theorists whom I consider here do not specify how this difference is to be arrived at or maintained. Thus Durkheim and Piaget never resolved the dilemma of how a morality of autonomy is to be derived from the traditional teaching of morality understood as submission to social authority. My aim is to expose the importance of this dilemma in the role of language in moral theory and in the relationships among Durkheim, Piaget, Kohlberg, and Habermas.

Durkheim on Language and Morality

Durkheim held that social life was made up entirely of *representations* (Durkheim [1903] 1982). These representations are both conscious and unconscious, and partly autonomous relative to the human agent even though they cannot exist apart from the mental life of agents (Durkheim [1893] 1933: 97; [1912] 1965: 31, 264; [1924] 1974: 1–31; [1925] 1961: 277; [1938] 1977: 342–348). He created a new epistemology called "renovated rationalism" as a tool for understanding these phenomena (see Durkheim [1912] 1965: 31; [1955] 1938: 2; Bouglé 1938: 24; Strickwerda 1982; Mestrovic 1985). Unlike traditional rationalism, renovated rationalism claims that reason is a collective and impersonal product of historical development. Reason is not an *a priori* faculty for Durkheim, but is a social faculty; it varies in relation to social structure. Unlike empiricism and pragmatism, renovated rationalism insists, nevertheless, that truth is permanent and fixed (see especially Durkheim [1955] 1983). In short, Durkheim attempted to straddle both sides of some version of what has come to be known as the object–subject debate (Cortese and Mestrovic 1989).

The objective–subjective distinction in the discovery of social reality is crucial to my discussion on language and morality. Durkheim treated the "subjective" as that which refers to something that occurs solely in the realm of ideas; the "objective" relates to "real," that is, material events. Durkheim ([1903] 1982) distinguished between objective (material) and subjective (non-material) dimensions of social facts. Morality is problematic because it is simultaneously objective and subjective. Law and its processes (e.g., due process, jury deliberation, sentencing) can be understood as examples of "objective" morality. Morality, however, is not totally objective:

> Not all of morality is formulated in clear precepts. The greater part is diffused. There is a large collective life which is at liberty; all sorts of currents come, go, circulate everywhere, cross and mingle in a thousand different ways, and just because they are constantly mobile are never crystalized in an objective form. (Durkheim [1897] 1951: 315)

The point is that morality can also be an intersubjective phenomenon that can exist in the consciousness of individuals as well as between them.

Durkheim's recognition and use of both subjective and objective social facts is especially evident in his dualistic conceptualization of language (Cortese and Mestrovic 1989). "The ideas which correspond to the diverse elements of language are thus collective representations" (Durkheim [1912] 1965: 485). A simple one-to-one correspondence between language and ideas does not exist. Language necessarily distorts "reality" because as we use it we manipulate language to our individual needs and preferences. Durkheim referred to this process as the "individualization" of language. The distinction between the collective and private versions of language, for Durkheim, parallels the distinction between the sacred and the profane. Collective representations are somewhat paradoxical:

> Each of us sees them after as his own fashion. There are some which escape us completely and remain outside of our circle of vision; there are others of which we perceive certain aspects only. There are even a great many which we pervert in holding, for as they are collective by nature, they cannot become individualized without being retouched, modified, and consequently falsified. (Durkheim [1912] 1965: 484)

For Durkheim, the capacity to use language and concepts are what distinguishes humans from animals ([1912] 1965: 487). Although, since Durkheim's time, it is now debatable whether animals can use language (e.g., chimpanzees have been trained to link symbols and to construct sentences), it appears to be the case that animals cannot create language. Durkheim suggested that concepts do not originate within individuals but are collective in nature ([1912] 1965: 482). The collective aspect of language carries within itself a résumé of the "wisdom of science which the group has accumulated in the course of centuries" ([1912] 1965: 484). Hence "a concept is not my concept; I hold it in common with other men. . . . it is the work of the community" ([1912] 1965: 481).

To view language as a social fact is to treat it as an "impersonal representation" ([1912] 1965: 482). Like all social facts (see Durkheim's *Rules*, [1903] 1982), language exerts constraint, is general, and exists independently of its personal manifestations in speech. "Language can be considered a 'thing' [social fact] separate from our use of it as individuals, because it is inherited entirely from the other speakers who teach it to us and it is not our product" (Dineen 1967: 194). Durkheim pointed to the difference between the collective and private aspects of language:

> There are scarcely any words among those which we usually employ whose meaning does not pass, to a greater or less extent, the limits of our personal experience. . . . Thus there is a great deal of knowledge condensed in the word which I never collected, and which is not individual; it even surpasses me to such an extent that I cannot even completely appropriate all its results. ([1912] 1965: 483)

Like William James and the other pragmatists, Durkheim ([1938] 1977: 344; [1955] 1983) wrote that thought is a stream of consciousness and that prior to language, the world is chaos. However, unlike the pragmatists, whom he criticized in *Pragmatism and Sociology* ([1955] 1983), Durkheim argued that "we owe to language *[langue]* the introduction into our mind of distinctness and logical organization" ([1938] 1977: 345). Accordingly, language, as a social fact, is characterized by constraint *(contrainte)*, implying violence, coercion, and force (Cortese and Mestrovic 1989). That is, language is violence against thought considered as a stream of consciousness. It places structure on disorder:

> It is words that introduce distinctions into the thread of our thinking. For the word is a discrete entity; it has a definite individuality and sharply defined limits. . . . In a sense, language does violence to thought; it denatures it and mutilates it since it expresses in discontinuous terms what is essentially continuous. (Durkheim [1938] 1977: 344)

Consequently, Durkheim believed that "the concept is an essentially impersonal representation; . . . through it . . . human intelligences communicate" ([1912] 1965: 482) and that:

> Thinking conceptually is not simply isolating and grouping together the common characteristics of a certain number of objects; it is relating the variable to the permanent, the individual to the social ([1912] 1965: 487).

Durkheim's dualistic conceptualization of language explains why he considered the etymology of language salient to the teaching of morality (see Durkheim [1938] 1977: 342–348). The core of morality is duty and a sense of obligation that overrides purely selfish, private, egotistic motives (Cortese and Mestrovic 1989). Since language is a social fact, it must be understood in terms of its obligatory, necessitating, coercive qualities. After all, from infancy on, the adult world transforms the child's babbling and private idiosyncratic speech—what Piaget called "egocentric language"— into talk that can be used for communication, basically by imposing the collective aspects of language on the child.

Piaget's Interpretation of Durkheim

Like Durkheim and his disciples, Piaget was an active member of the French Philosophical Society and took part in their scholarly debates, some of which are published in the *Bulletin de la Societé Française de Philosophie* (Cortese and Mestrovic 1989). The philosopher, André Lalande, who published the *Vocabulaire technique et critique de la philosophie* ([1926] 1980), was an important influence on both Durkheim and Piaget, and frequently mentioned both men in this famous dictionary. Nevertheless, the effect of the French Philosophical Society on sociological theory has been thoroughly neglected. In this section, I would like to examine the explicit use of Durkheim in Piaget's *Moral Judgment of the Child* ([1932] 1965) and the implicit influence of Durkheim upon Piaget's *Language and Thought of the Child* (1926). I will expand on the links between linguistics and morality established in the previous section and set up the context by which Kohlberg and Habermas's relationships to Piaget and Durkheim may be evaluated.

Piaget noted the impact on his own work of Durkheim and his follower, Paul Fauconnet, particularly the latter's still untranslated book, *La responsabilité* (1920):

> For ourselves we know of no thesis so well suited as this doctrine of Durkheim's and Fauconnet's to throw light on the problems raised by the affirmation of the moral unity of society. . . . The great lesson of comparative sociology is that there exist at least two types of responsibility—one objective and communicable, the other subjective and individual, and that social evolution has gradually caused the second to predominate. ([1932] 1965: 333)

This important passage directly links Durkheim to Piaget's theory of moral development (Cortese and Mestrovic 1989). What attracted Piaget to Durkheim and Fauconnet's moral theory was the dualistic assertion of invariability and directed structural evolution. In addition, Piaget agreed with "the main thesis of Durkheim's doctrine, i.e., the explanation of morality by social life, and the interpretation of its changes in terms of the varying structure of society" ([1932] 1965: 344). This sociological aspect of Piaget's developmental theory has certainly been neglected.

Recall that Piaget proposed two moralities in the child, that of constraint and heteronomy (which Piaget called "objective") versus that of cooperation and autonomy (which Piaget called "subjective"). Heteronomy is the subjection of an individual to the authority or guidance of another (Piaget [1932] 1965). He connected these concepts to several Durkheimian dualisms. In societies characterized by mechanical solidarity, morality rests on consensus and repressive law, not justice. In societies characterized by organic solidarity, morality rests on "the cult of the individual," restitutive law, and justice: "The task of the most advanced societies is, then, a work of justice. . . . Just as ancient peoples needed, above all, a common faith to live by, so we need justice" (Durkheim [1893] 1933: 388). Piaget compared the initial morality of children and their submissive attitude toward adults to the morality characteristic of mechanical solidarity (Cortese and Mestrovic 1989). Children develop a morality based on justice in a manner analogous to the process of societies' development:

> The adult who is under the dominion of unilateral respect for the "Elders" and for tradition is really behaving like a child. It may even be maintained that the realism of primitive conceptions of crime and punishment is, in certain respects, an infantile reaction. (Piaget [1932] 1965: 340)

The progression of children's development reflects the evolution of societies from forced conformity to differentiation, diminished supervision, autonomy, and cooperation.

Piaget studied an intriguing dilemma rooted in any attempt to institute the morality of autonomy in children. How does one permit the liberty of conscience if education stems from the traditional model and relies on methods that are essentially those of authority? Piaget never completely resolved this dilemma. Pure subjectivism contests constraint and duty, but these are key elements of morality. On the other hand, pure objectivism denies autonomy and rational individual intention and interpretation, which are also critical aspects of morality. Piaget was ingenious in finding passages in Durkheim's text that support both views—that morality is mere compliance with public opinion and the view that morality involves obedience to society "as it really is" even if that means ignoring public opinion:

> One must make one's choice between these two solutions. . . . For either society is one, and all social processes, including cooperation, are to be assimilated to pure constraint alone, in which case right is bound to be determined by public opinion and traditional use; or else a distinction must be made between actual and ideal society. . . . [But] how, we would ask, is it possible to distinguish between society as it is and society as it is tending to become? (Piaget [1932] 1965: 346)

What is popular is not always right, and what is right is not always popular.

Piaget analyzed the thorn that continues to bother moral theory and Durkheimian scholarship. Giddens (1986) has maintained that the Parsonian focus on the allegedly Durkheimian problem of order and linkage between Durkheim and Hobbes are false. Alexander (1982) has noted that Durkheim should still be regarded in the context of an overriding concern with social order, without addressing the dilemma Piaget uncovered, that such a concern would seem to run contrary to establishing a morality of autonomy. Giddens (1971) and Nisbet (1974) fueled this debate by adding that Durkheim ambiguously advocated both a type of "moral individualism" and submission to authority. As Giddens (1971: 496) stated, Durkheim's thought "would appear to lead to a self-determination of the individual; it also goes hand in hand with a widening of the powers of the state to subject the individual to its authority."

Kohlberg disregarded Piaget's focus on this dilemma altogether, and banished Durkheimian thought as conformist morality. According to Kohlberg (1981b), Durkheim's theory argues that the social psychological origins of morality are to be found in the collective beliefs of the group, as these form a system above the beliefs of individuals. But there was much more to Durkheim's model of morality than that, and Piaget was much more sensitive to Durkheim's thought than Kohlberg has been.

Actually, it is not evident that one must choose between these two solutions. A middle ground is feasible, and in that regard one could argue that Durkheim's theory is a balanced one. After all, Durkheim portrayed the division of labor as a reconciliation of the necessities of social cohesion with individualism ([1893] 1933: 395). Piaget even assumed that in moral development, previous stages are not entirely abandoned (i.e., the presumption of hierarchial integration). But these unresolved tensions become most obvious when one applies linguistics to moral theory. Parallel to his analogy between children and primitives, Piaget associated the language of children prior to age eight with "savages and imbeciles." He denied that young children use language mainly to communicate thought. Instead, children sometimes talk to themselves, express commands and desires, and in general, do not try to be objective in their explanations. Piaget regarded this language as "egocentric" since the child "does not bother to know to whom he is speaking nor whether he is being listened to" (1926: 40). Like Durkheim, Piaget proposed a dualism between "egocentric" and "socialized" thought and language. In egocentricity, "we give rein to our imagination" but "when we think socially, we are far more obedient to the imperative to truth" (1926: 124).

There is some vagueness in Piaget's terms regarding moral and linguistic development. Concerning moral judgment, he called the first stage "objective" and the second "subjective," but reversed the order of these labels with regard to linguistic development. However, Piaget, like Durkheim, argued that language is objective when it is communicable, which is to say, when it is "impersonal" and "social" (1926: 271). This linguistic objectivity is subject to constraints, particularly social constraints. Thus Piaget refuted his own claim that one must choose between constraint and cooperation. He implicitly repeated the Durkheimian position that superior moral development is contingent upon transcending egoism and being forced to acknowledge social constraints. Such social constraints are clearly different from the constraints of primitive and child morality, but they are constraints, nonetheless.

This problem is significant for the agenda that needs to be addressed with regard to the sociological import of moral theory. And it sets the context for what follows.

Conclusion

The role of language in moral theory is critical for Durkheim. In fact, he argued that the etymology of language is significant in the teaching of morality. Durkheim maintained that language is a social fact and proposed a dualistic conception of language: the private versus the collective. Piaget's cognitive-structural framework of moral development is indebted to Durkheim. I have attempted to illustrate the sociological implications of Piaget's theory. Kohlberg, in turn, created a six-stage theory of moral reasoning based on the basic assumptions of Piaget's approach. Descriptions of Kohlberg's six stages are provided in the next chapter. Kohlberg's writings have justified Habermas's affirming that universalistic critical thought is grounded in the normal development of the human mind. In Chapter 7, the salience of the collective aspect of language as advanced by Durkheim is the basis of a critique of Kohlberg's model of moral development and Habermas's theory of communicative ethics. Durkheim's concept of justice was examined in relation to Piaget. I will do the same for Kohlberg and Habermas.

In the next chapter, I apply the epistemological distinction between subject and object to the sociology of knowledge. The sociology of knowledge is crucial to the thrust of this book because it supports my argument that morality must be bound to a particular cultural or sociohistorical context. Morality contains no intrinsic laws of development. Its validity has no ultimate basis. Instead, moral systems prosper or fail within specific cultural and historical settings.

3

The Sociology of Knowledge and Moral Development

"We care more for skill than for the disposition to use it well."
—*Immanuel Kant*, Lectures on Ethics

"Knowledge . . . obeys no inherent law of development. Whether it flourishes or stagnates . . . are questions of history. This knowledge, like all other, is context-bound."
—*William Perdue*, Sociological Theory

Durkheim and Piaget's concerns with the contradictory elements of moral reality—objective versus subjective, constraint versus autonomy, individual rights versus group rights—are similar to those of Husserl, Lukacs, Engels, and Marx, who were interested in the problem of the objectivity of knowledge and the development of human consciousness. These theorists influenced Karl Mannheim, who is viewed as being the key intellectual forefather of the sociology of knowledge. This chapter examines Mannheim's concepts of ideology, utopia, and relationism. Mannheim argued that critical reasoning permits relative autonomy from determinism. This crucial presupposition can be seen in Kohlberg's six-stage theory of moral reasoning. Kohlberg represents an attempt to expand on Mannheim's recognition that consciousness is linked to the social context of human development.

In Chapter 1, the philosophical assumptions and epistemological underpinnings of the cognitive development approach to morality were examined. This included a look at Kant's ethical system and his focus on justice through the Categorical Imperative. Kant's rational model of moral action was picked up by Piaget, who

43

stressed the universality of moral stages. John Rawls' theory of justice reflects the formalism of Kant and Piaget. Rawls also received attention in Chapter 1 because his framework gives Kohlberg's theory a normative philosophic grounding. In this chapter, I provide descriptions of Kohlberg's six stages of moral reasoning. This is important because the structure and substance of the stages are the heart of Kohlberg's theory of moral development. It will become evident that Kohlberg's emphasis on justice mirrors that of Kant, Piaget, and Rawls.

Mannheim: Ideology and Utopia

Mannheim is credited with pioneering the sociology of knowledge *(Wissenssoziologie)*, especially in his *Ideology and Utopia* ([1936] 1971). Systematic consideration of social factors in the aquisition, diffusion, and growth of knowledge has its two main roots in French and German sociological thought. The French branch is above all Durkheim and is derived from an ethnographic background that stressed the range of variation among different groups of people— variation in moral, social, and especially cognitive structure. In *The Elementary Forms of Religious Life*, Durkheim ([1912] 1965) provided a bold analysis of the social origins of the fundamental categories of thought.

German historicism and left-wing Hegelianism also influenced Mannheim's thought. The main German antecedents of the sociology of knowledge are found among the immediate forerunners of Mannheim: Marx, Lukacs, and especially Engels. To be sure, these various influences included conflicting perspectives; yet all were essentially concerned with the developing, "produced" character of knowledge situated in history. Mannheim was particularly interested in the transition from ideology to knowledge, and viewed the social and especially the class structure as strong determinants of the categorization of knowledge. Consequently, the task of the sociology of knowledge was to analyze, without regard for class bias, all of the factors in the existing social situation which may influence thought. This results in a dynamic conception of knowledge.

The new conception of the role of knowledge shifted action from the realm of "necessity" to that of "freedom." Mannheim looked at how conflicting social groups initiated reflective thought, emphasizing empirical sociology vis-à-vis historical determinism. Through the influence of Dilthey, Rickert, Troeltsch, Weber, and Neo-Kantians from the Southwest, or Baden, school, Mannheim emphasized affectional-volitional elements in the formation of thought. From the phenomenologists—Husserl, Jaspers, Heidegger, and especially Scheler, Mannheim stressed the accurate observation of facts "given" in direct experience. Given the diversity of Mannheim's intellectual influences, it is not difficult to understand the eclecticism and fundamental instability in his conceptual framework.

Mannheim derived much of his model of the sociology of knowledge from his analysis of the concept *ideology.* "Awareness of ideological thought comes when an adversary's assertions are regarded as untrue by virtue of their determination of his life situation" (Merton [1949] 1968: 546). Because such distortions are not intentional, an ideology is not a lie. Sometimes ideology is particular, at other times the entire system of thought is ideological. A particular ideology assumes that individuals share common criteria of validity. In contrast, a total ideology is a mode of thought that is bound to a life situation (i.e., a strong correspondence between a social setting and a system of thought). The development from a particular to a total ideology results in a problem of false consciousness (i.e., how a totally distorted mind that falsified all within its range could ever have arisen). The analysis of particular and total ideologies was merged in Marxism, which shifted the unit of analysis from the psychological to the sociological.

The shift from a "special" to a "general" formulation of the concept of ideology was necessary for the emergence of a sociology of knowledge. In the special formulation, only adversaries' thought is regarded as totally a function of their social position. But with a general formulation, the thought of all social groups is so regarded. Therefore, the theory of ideology could develop into the sociology of knowledge. Mannheim was noted for dropping the rhetoric of ideology and working toward a scientific study of cognition and knowledge. While the theory of ideology is a political discipline, the sociology of knowledge is a cognitive one. As we shall see later, Kohlberg and Habermas's emphasis on cognition is precisely what makes their theories of moral reasoning and communication so salient for the sociology of knowledge.

According to Merton, there are two main branches of the sociology of knowledge: theory and "an historico-sociological method of research" ([1949] 1968: 548). The theoretical component involves empirical investigation through description and structural analysis of the ways in which culture and social relationships influence cognition. The methodological part concerns the development of procedures for constructing the ideal types implied in the structure of reasoning found in various social strata. Kohlberg's theory and methodology have addressed both of these closely related components of the sociology of knowledge.

It is only when one comes into contact with radically different modes of thought that one begins to question one's own forms of thought. Rapid social change results in doubting and reexamination of what was formerly taken for granted. Mannheim (1967) sought to establish a link between cognition and social structure; even the categories under which experiences are subsumed, collected, and ordered vary according to the social position of the observer. The social order is seen as legitimate and proper, not problematic. Mannheim has been credited with relating several types of utopian mentality to the particular social location of their protagonists.

What constitutes knowledge? Mannheim used the term inconsistently. "Knowledge" ranged from rigorous positive science to any type of assertion or any mode of thought resulting from folk belief. He viewed knowledge as existentially determined, but not in terms of a mechanical cause–effect sequence. Empirical investigation could test the degree of covariation between life situation and thought process.

Mannheim's conception of knowledge as ideology led to an epistemology of radical relativism. "Whatever is found true under certain conditions should not be assumed to be true universally or without limits and conditions" (Merton [1949] 1968: 559). Mannheim sought to provide grounds for the validity of knowledge within the confines of given frameworks. He escaped from the problem of relativism by adherence to the "classless position" of the "socially unattached intellectuals" (socialfreischwebende Intelligenz). Intellectuals provided evaluation, reliability, and synthesis regarding the sociology of knowledge. Validity was achieved through the diverse life experiences of detached intellectuals. But a problem remained: Which intellectual position was correct when there was a lack of consensus, a competition between views? This was a major paradox left unresolved by Mannheim. But Mannheim also left behind an insightful analysis that linked thought with experience: Knowledge was understandable only in terms of non-cognitive experience, including the effect of social structure in guiding and activating thought.

The problem of reliable knowledge had two solutions. The first one was to argue that all knowledge was relative. This was not satisfactory for Mannheim; consequently, he assumed a position of relationism. This meant an acceptance and study of the influence of social and historical contexts upon the formulation of ideas. But this also included the recognition that one can and must discriminate between valid and erroneous claims to knowledge. The education of intellectuals allowed them to transcend class viewpoints. Although Marx shared a background in German historicism with Mannheim, Marx was not interested in problems of relativism, the starting-point for Mannheim, for whom the intellectuals' major task was to evaluate and reconcile the particular ideologies of the political arena. Although knowledge is relative, within a particular belief system there are intersubjective rules that permit the construction of valid knowledge and the refutation of erroneous hypotheses.

Moral Theory and the Sociology of Knowledge

Mannheim's conception of human nature as reason, self-reflection, and intention is generally consistent with the epistemological assumptions of the cognitive-structural frameworks of Piaget and Kohlberg, which Habermas takes over. Mannheim opposed ideology, the systems of thought protected by dominant groups which hide or obfuscate actual conditions and thereby maintain and promote the status quo. He countered with utopian systems of thought held by oppressed groups trying to change society. Utopian thought provided a "rationally justifiable system of ideas to legitimate and direct change" (Perdue 1986: 392).

This type of cognitive and ethical model, as formulated by Mannheim, can be traced from Kant to Piaget, Kohlberg, and Habermas. For example, the meaning of Habermas's conception of "legitimation," which was taken from Weber, is essentially that of Mannheim's "ideology." Consequently, the types of problems raised here about Kant (Chapter 1), Durkheim (Chapter 2), Piaget (Chapters 1 and 2), Kohlberg (Chapters 4 and 6), and Habermas (Chapter 7) also haunted Mannheim. Mannheim's significant distinction between "relative" and "relational" allows the actor to bracket the sociohistorical context of a moral dilemma and evaluate the opposing sides in hopes of getting close to truth. Mannheim recognized the structural constraints on thought but vaguely concluded that knowledge is anchored by social position. Kohlberg and Habermas attempted to expand on this and supersede the social context through the development of reason.

Mannheim's integration of subjective and objective forces that stimulate human knowledge is analogous to the reconciliation of idealism and materialism that caused such trouble for Kant, Schopenhauer, Durkheim, and a host of others. On the one hand, human spirit and ideas are extemporaneous, unlimited, and unforeseeable. On the other hand, social conditioning and biological factors cannot be denied. A sociology of knowledge could take care of this paradox and provide a scientific basis for the study of society. No knowledge is value-free; hence, truth always refers to a particular sociohistorical context. Knowledge is not metaphysical, but of this world, and its form reveals something about the status of the holder of knowledge. According to Mannheim, social classes see reality from different vantage points. These world-views are collective, not individual, and each has different criteria for "truth." Applying this point to moral theory, one may see that each group has its own moral system, a belief structure for what ought to be, as well as what is.

Mannheim ([1936] 1971) was fully aware that issues of morality, truth, and knowledge are often found in political conflict. He used the adjective "Utopian" to refer to total systems of thought held by oppressed classes trying to change society. This is similar to the concept of "communicative action" by Habermas, where the actor is motivated by autonomy rather than heteronomy. Accordingly, the goal of social thought is to develop a rationally, and hence universally, defendable structure of ideas to legitimate change and transform society. This point weaves throughout the writings of Kant, Piaget, Mannheim, Kohlberg, and Habermas.

Like philosophers of science (e.g., Flew, 1985; Trigg, 1985) who refused to grant that cultural relativism eliminated objective truth (see Chapter 2), Mannheim went beyond merely stating that there are different truths. When opposing perspectives are brought forward on the same issue, evaluations must be made regarding the differential validity of these positions. Simply put, one stance may be more accurate than another. Utopian ideas in one context may be regarded as ideological in another. Mannheim labored over the content of ideas and their link to a total structure of cognition. Yet, in presenting the significant questions of differences in cognitive structures, he did little more than assert that "knowledge" is determined by social position (Perdue 1986). Mannheim described particular classes and social movements, illustrating how their systems of thought differ. But he rarely focused on the actual material conditions that produced ideological and utopian viewpoints.

The Sociopolitical Base for Knowledge

Mannheim was interested in problems of interpretation, epistemology, and especially types of knowledge. He examined the social forces that contributed to the emergence and molding of particular kinds of knowledge (Purdue 1986). Mannheim also focused on the structural formation of personality and as mentioned in the previous section in *Ideology and Utopia* ([1936] 1971) held a conception of human nature as one of reason, mediation, and self-reflection. In fact, self-awareness, critical reasoning, and scientific method assume an acknowledgment of the relationship between cognitive structure and social structure. This does not mean that value stances are meaningless or that "knowledge" is a false reality. Instead, if one operates with an awareness of social life, one is able to grasp the often latent aspects of thought within society. Not only do we have the capacity of self-reflection, but such awareness occurs within a particular context or situation. If this happens, then systematic understanding of society is possible.

Mannheim ([1936] 1971: 47) seemed to have reached a synthesized understanding of subjective and objective reality, of free will and determinism, when he stated: "The inner connection between our role, our motivations, and our type and manner of experiencing the world suddenly dawns upon us." Mannheim insisted that rationality allows us relative autonomy from determinism, an important assumption echoed by Piaget, Kohlberg, and Habermas. Critical rationality permits simultaneous comprehension of subject, object, and the sociohistorical context. As in Marx, class conflict and tensions between systems of thought are a major theme throughout much of Mannheim's work. Different classes hold different, and often contradictory, systems of belief and related value stances. But unlike Marx, who argued that the ideas of the ruling class were dominant, Mannheim stressed the importance of the ideas of scholars, intellectuals, and the educated, who came from all classes. The great range of the intellectual class resulted in a diversity of often conflicting ideas. Similarly, subcultural groups based on ethnicity, race, or religion support different and sometimes contradictory systems of ethical thought, each of which are valid within its particular sociohistorical and cultural setting. This is the major point that I wish to bring against the attempts to universalize morality by Kant, Piaget, Kohlberg, and Habermas.

In sum, the sociology of knowledge focused on epistemology and the empirical analysis of the manner in which forms of social life affect the production of ideas. Giddens argued that Mannheim's "thesis that the sociology of knowledge is relationist rather than relativistic comes down to little more than an unsubstantiated assertion." Furthermore, "Mannheim never seems to have made up his mind about what counts as a valid claim to knowledge, or at least where the boundary lies between knowledge and mere partisan belief" (Giddens 1979: 172, 173). These same types of problems also affect the cogency of Kohlberg's and Habermas's cases. The intellectual sources that influenced Kohlberg and Habermas included most of those with whom Mannheim was concerned. Let us now shift to a contemporary framework for the sociology of knowledge, as developed in the work of Kohlberg.

Kohlberg's Six Stages of Moral Reasoning

Kohlberg (1984) has noted that his moral dilemmas address the problem of procedural justice, a concern that is only clearly distinguishable in higher-stage moral judgments. Procedural justice often represents the considerations that moral philosophers treat as "validity checks" on moral reasoning. Such checks are based on balancing differing perspectives or making judgments reversible (i.e., employing the Golden Rule) and universal (i.e., employing Kant's Categorical Imperative). Reversibility implies the question: "Would you judge this action as fair if you were in the other person's shoes?". The ability to be universalized implies the question: "Would you judge this action right if everyone were to do it?"

In the descriptions of his stages that follow, I employ Kohlberg's (1984) discussion of stage-specific sociomoral perspectives on norms in general and upon the justice operations of equality, equity, reciprocity, prescriptive role taking, and universalizability.

Stage 1: Heteronomous Morality

Stage 1 is based on naive *moral realism*. There is a literal reification of the moral significance of an act such that its rightness or wrongness is viewed as a real, inherent, and permanent quality of the action. A parallel position is the perspective that color and mass are regarded as inherent qualities of objects. Moral realism at Stage 1 is consistent with the premise that moral decisions are self-evident and require little or no justification beyond citing rules and assigning labels. For example, telling on one's sibling is bad because that is labelled "tattle-taling," "ratting," or "squealing." A further example: Breaking into the druggist's shop is wrong because "you're not supposed to steal." Punishment is automatically connected with a forbidden behavior and is viewed as the reason why an action is considered bad. For example, "You shouldn't take a cookie from the cookie jar because you'll get spanked." Similarly, there is a lack of mediating concepts, such as intentionality, through which the particular circumstances of the situation may change its moral significance. Consequently, moral rules and labels are taken in a literal and absolute manner.

Justice is characterized by rigid equality, not equity. Morality tends to be equated with power. Characteristics of persons that shape their authority, power, or moral worth tend to be physicalistic or categorical. For example, "Dad is the boss because he's bigger." Another example: "You should steal to save a life if it's Betsy Ross; she made the flag." Moral realism connotes an inability to distinguish multiple views on dilemmas. This implies that there is a single definition of the situation and only one right response to it. There is no conflict or disagreement between individual's perceptions of the moral dilemma regardless of power differences between them. Kohlberg's Stage 1 is equivalent to Piaget's morality of heteronomy; the goodness or badness of an action is determined by authority rather than by cooperation among equal individuals.

Norms, from the perspective of Stage 1, are exact rules not related to expectations of any individuals, including the self. Rather, norms are understood as categories of good and bad behavior. Such categories identify the moral character of types of action (e.g., stealing is always wrong) and types of persons (e.g., nice girls, good boys, famous persons, con men). According to Stage 1, *equality* is a rigid coordination of those individuals considered to be within a single category of actors or persons. Consequently, discriminating treatment of those within a less valued category is justifiable. Reciprocity is identified as the exchange of goods or actions without concern for the psychological valuing of goods or actions by self or other. This perspective is based on tit-for-tat reciprocity (e.g., An eye for eye, and a tooth for a tooth). Stage 1 is egocentric and heteronomous, but lacks the operations of equity and prescriptive role taking. In short, the unharmonious use of reciprocity and equality characterizes this stage. A type of universalizability emerges in which a law, norm, or rule is generalized without a single concession, with the possible exception of the authorities by whom the rules are constructed and enforced.

Stage 2: Instrumental Relativistic Morality

A particular kind of individualistic perspective characterizes moral reasoning at Stage 2. There is recognition that every individual has his/her own welfare to seek and protect; conflicts between individual interests may occur. A stance of moral relativism emerges from the claim that various persons can have different, yet equally valid justification for their notions of justice. There is respect for the ethical legitimacy of acting on the basis of one's own interests. Multiple outlooks on a situation are acknowledged. "Good" action is relative: (1) to the particular situation and (b) to the individual's view of the situation. At Stage 2, a person judges an action to be right or wrong in terms of the action's capacity to maximize satisfaction of one's own desires and needs while simultaneously minimizing negative consequences to the self. The major objective of the actor is to pragmatically pursue one's own interests. The presupposition that others operate on this premise leads to an expectation of instrumental exchange as a vehicle through which actors can arrange their actions for mutual good. Consequently, the moral realism of Stage 1 is eclipsed, but the extreme relativism of Stage 2 results in an inability to provide a tool for resolving opposing claims or setting priorities on conflicting desires and needs.

According to Stage 2, norms are psychological expectations of individual selves. They are criteria for regulating behavior and fulfilling individual desires. Morality is relativistic; normative expectations maintain an equilibrium through exchange. The notion of *equality* at Stage 2 acknowledges the legitimacy of seeking to satisfy desires by individuals through the exchange of goods and actions with others. All individual needs and interests are considered equally legitimate; actions are not inherently right or wrong. *Reciprocity* at Stage 2 involves a conception of concrete exchange of equal goods or values in addressing the needs of the self and the other. The operations of reciprocity and equality are coordinated here, unlike Stage 1. At Stage 2, for example, one can reason that a child has the right to refuse a parent's request for the money that the child earned through work. And if a parent wants money, then s/he should earn it him/herself. The operation of equity is centered on the needs, not the intentions, of individuals. For example, it may be right for poor people to steal because they need food.

Prescriptive role taking at Stage 2 recognizes the fact that the actor could have needs similar to others (e.g., "If I were Heinz and needed the drug for my wife as he did, then I too would steal it").

While various moral stances are symmetrical at Stage 2 since the self can grasp the needs and behavior of other actors, they are not coordinated enough to resolve conflicts between viewpoints. The idea of the universalizable is revealed by a recognition of the need to constrain all deviant behavior of naturally self-interested actors. The point is that if departure from norms is permitted for one, then it would only be fair that others also deviate. But this situation may result in a condition whereby the fair pursuit of self-interest and fair exchange is subverted. For example, those who break the law should be punished, because if they are not punished, others may attempt to get away with breaking the law.

Stage 3: Interpersonally Normative Morality

According to this stage, the separate views of actors are integrated into a third-person perspective, that of mutually trusting relationships among people, which is assimilated into a set of shared moral norms according to which actors are expected to live. Such moral norms and expectations go beyond particular persons and situations. Norms at Stage 3 are distinct from rules at Stage 1: the former symbolize a synthesis of views that have been understood as separate, a consensus on what constitutes a "good" person. Being "nice" becomes important. On the other hand, rules at Stage 1 fail to distinguish different individual positions. The primacy of shared norms at Stage 3 represents a focus on right or wrong motives as indicative of general personal morality. There is also a strong concern with being good, altruistic, and prosocial. The recognition of the salience of individual motives also differentiates Stage 3 norms from Stage 1 rules. Stage 3 is characterized by the desire to obtain social approval and maintain interpersonal trust.

At Stage 3, justice is seen as role taking by the Golden Rule—do unto others as you would have others do unto you. Logically, this implies the balancing of self-regard and other perspectives. Stage 3 transcends the reciprocal exchanges of Stage 2 by subjecting it to critique by reference to a superordinate or shared norm against which its fairness can be evaluated. In short, reciprocal exchange is not necessarily just, but must be supported or rejected on the basis of ethical standards of good conduct that exist independent of the specific content of any reciprocal exchange.

Norms are recognized as shared expectations within a relationship. They function to promote loyalty, trust, and caring between persons and to maintain relationships and groups. These relational norms are understood as obligatory. The operation of reciprocity creates an "economic" notion of obligation as a form of debt; the other has given a value or something valuable to the self, and the self cannot end this imbalance by a simple one-to-one exchange but instead internalizes feelings of gratitude and loyalty, and a need to reciprocate. Kohlberg notes, as an example, a response to the question: "Is it a duty for Heinz to steal?" The subject replies: "If I was Heinz, I would have stolen the drug for my wife. You cannot put a price on love; no amount of gifts make love. You cannot put a price on life either." Clearly, the subject has gone beyond the instrumental relativism and concrete equal exchange of Stage 2 by placing an emphasis on obligation and responsibility to the relationship. This permits one to grasp reciprocity as surpassing concrete conceptions of equal exchange in order to affirm notions of gratitude, debt, and obligation, the mutuality of expectations and relationships. Reciprocity, at this stage, creates an image of exchange whereby those who are good or have worked hard are deserving of their just rewards.

At Stage 3, the notion of equality develops a class of actors who should be treated equally because of their good motives and status as "good role occupants." The notion of equity points to the possibility that actors sometimes deserve to be exempted from the generally negative reaction to deviant behavior, stemming from the admission of mitigating circumstances and an appreciation of good intentions. The Stage 3 notions of reciprocity, equality, and equity are adapted and linked to a prescriptive role-taking operation. For example, "It's all right for Heinz to steal the drug because the druggist is heartless in ignoring Heinz's wife's right to live." A further example: "The judge should be lenient with Heinz because he has suffered enough and didn't want to steal."

The operation of balancing perspectives, or prescriptive role taking, is the clear use of the Golden Rule for the first time at Stage 3. It may be communicated by the thought that an action is good from one's own particular perspective if one could accept it as good from another perspective. Hence, the Golden Rule may be a positive prescription. For example, "You should help to save someone's life, because if you were they, you would want to help save your life." How universalizing at Stage 3 is conceptualized is shown in the following statement: "Everyone should obey the law because without it immoral people would create societal disorder." This universalistic operation reveals a proclivity to constrain deviant behavior that would hamper the actions and the realizing of the intentions of moral individuals (those who are loyal, fair, just, and so on). Consequently, there is a strong apprehension about any disorganization that would obstruct a community of virtuous actors.

Stage 4: Social System Morality

The actor at Stage 4 internalizes societal norms and assumes the stance of a generalized member of society. Such a position is supported by the notion of the social system as a coherent set of codes and regulations and procedures that promote equality for each actor. The quest for individual interests is regarded as justifiable only if it fits within the sociomoral system as a whole. The unofficially shared norms of Stage 3 are classified at Stage 4 for greater fairness and regularity. The common good is advanced through official institutions and roles within a social structure that resolves opposing rights and assertions. There is recognition that there can be major disagreement even between good role occupants. This admission necessitates the construction of a series of codified procedures for judging such conflicts.

A viewpoint emerges from a sociolegal and religious order resulting in the systematic arrangement of institutionalized laws, rules, and practices. On the other hand, there may be a belief in some higher moral or religious authority incorporated in the individual conscience, which may clash with practical or institutionalized law. Internal conscience or moral law, in this context, is equivalent to some system of natural or divine law. In other words, moral judgments, at this stage, are based on their agreement with legal, social, moral, and religious institutions and belief systems.

Norms, at Stage 4, encourage cooperation or social contribution, function to regulate and maintain societal harmony, and are designed to avoid conflict. The notion of equality means "equality before the law." Individuals are equal in that the rights and duties of each individual are specified in terms of societal standards. For example, it is assumed that one should obey the law even if one does not believe in it, since law is thought to be based on general agreement, and one must respect what is considered to be right for the majority of people. The operation of equity, at Stage 4, is illustrated in the following: "The judge should be lenient to Heinz in order to demonstrate that the law can be fair or humane" and "Heinz should steal because the law cannot take into account all cases nor can it always be fair." Equity at Stage 4 makes clear exceptions to the general practical use of norms, on the principle that societal standards may not be adequately sensitive to incorporate particular individual circumstances or needs. This type of equity goes beyond the Stage 3 version since recognizing extenuating circumstances is the responsibility of the social system as a whole and of any of its members and not of a specific authority.

Reciprocity at Stage 4 is generally synonymous with the "norm of reciprocity" that connects the individual to the collectivity. There are tradeoffs; individuals receive benefits from living in society and being members of institutions. For example, "the druggist should have used his invention to benefit society" and "it is important to save another's life, because people must have some sense of responsibility for others for the sake of society."

Prescriptive role taking at Stage 4 attempts to strike a balance between societal standards and individual autonomy. For example, "Heinz should steal the drug but he should see that it is wrong in society's eyes and that he will have to be prepared to accept the consequences." The notion of universality, according to Stage 4, creates the concept of constraining deviant behavior in order to sustain basic respect for law and the soundness of social integration. This operation is expressed in the following statement: "One should obey the law because respect for the law will be destroyed if citizens feel they can break it just because they disagree with it."

Stage 5: Human Rights and Social Welfare Morality

At Stage 5, individuals reason through their rational moral positions and are cognizant of pancultural rights and values that anyone should use to construct a moral community. Like the preconventional level, postconventional morality is based on the perspective of the individual rather than taking the view of a member of society. The postconventional individual, however, takes a view that is universal or that of *any rational moral individual*. A person at Stage 5 is aware of the member-of-society perspective (Stage 4), but:

> questions and redefines it in terms of an individual moral perspective, so that social obligations are defined in ways that can be justified to any moral individual. An individual's commitment to basic morality or moral principles is seen as preceding, or being necessary for, his or her taking society's perspective or accepting society's laws and values (Kohlberg 1984: 178).

Thus, Stage 5 is called the "prior-to-society" perspective, referring to moral commitments or principles that are needed prior to the creation of a good or just society.

The legitimacy of actual laws and social systems can be judged in terms of the extent to which they preserve and protect basic human rights and values. The ideal society, at this stage, is a type of contract voluntarily agreed to by all actors in order to preserve the rights and promote the welfare of all members. Society is based on consensus and social cooperation. The major emphasis at Stage 5 is on social welfare and social rights.

Some rights are regarded as unbreakable by the society. Such rights may not be violated irrespective of voluntarily agreed-upon covenants. Every actor is obliged to make ethical decisions that are consistent with these rights—regardless of whether these decisions oppose actual laws or societal standards. There is recognition of the need to secure the rights of minorities, which could not be realized from the social position of Stage 4. An affirmative action philosophy is consistent with this type of reasoning. The focus on an appreciation for societal welfare mirrors a regulation of utilitarian philosophy in which social institutions, rules, or laws are judged in terms of their long-term benefits for each actor or group in society.

Norms are sought to serve and enhance individual rights and welfare at Stage 5; they are understood as being developed through unconstrained and consenting actors. The notion of equality acknowledges the basic equal rights and equal value of individuals as echoed in decisions concerning the fundamental priority of human life and freedom.

The operation of equity, at this stage, protects equality claims when norms, laws, or procedures are ignored or preclude essential human rights and deference to human life. For example, "It may not be wrong to break the law where its function was not to protect rights, but to protect infringements on them." Unlike earlier stages, where the aim of compensation for equity was some type of equality, at Stage 5 the aim of equity is to rectify the effects of the laws, norms, or regulations. This change in position is due to the evidence that, at Stage 5, notions of equality in life and freedom are basic premises in thinking, and function as the support for norms. This is in contrast to previous stages, where equality originates in norms, laws, and procedures and are utilized to support them.

The operation of reciprocity at Stage 5 creates the concept of transferring concrete or symbolic equivalents between voluntarily participating actors. In this sense, the major point is unconstrained conformity in a covenant, not merely the notion of the equivalence inferred by exchange. Stage 5 prescriptive role taking emphasizes the need to recognize the position of each actor who is involved in a particular social situation. In other words, each person is regarded and counted as an individual. For instance, "The doctor should take the woman's point of view as to whether she should live or not out of respect for her own sense of dignity and autonomy." Equality, equity, and reciprocity are synthesized to protect individual rights. An example of this applied to the context of equal opportunity follows: "Each person should have an equal chance to make her/his contribution to society and reap the appropriate benefits, even if s/he has different starting points or is disadvantaged." Universalizability, at Stage 5, supports a pancultural respect for the value of human life and liberty. Moral norms or laws should be all-inclusive or universalized for actors living in any human society.

Stage 6: Morality of Universalizable Ethical Principles

Stage 6 is based on a moral perspective that ideally every actor should assume, regarding others as free and autonomous persons. This translates as equal deliberation about the assertions or orientation of each actor affected by the moral dilemma to be resolved. Such prescriptive role taking is guided by regulations aimed to insure fairness, impartiality, or reversibility in role taking. These procedures are formalized in a variety of ways.

One such formulation is John Rawls' primary stance of choosing under a "Veil of Ignorance." According to the conception, the actor is not aware of which role in a situation or society s/he is to play, and must pick a principle or strategy with which s/he could best accept in any position, especially the circumstances of the person(s) most disadvantaged in the society (See Chapter 1).

Another formulation is that of reversibility or "moral musical chairs," a second-order application of the Golden Rule. In every moral situation, each actor should assume the perspective of the other in arguing his/her claim. A third element is framed by focusing on actual dialogue, what Habermas designates as an "ideal communication situation"—the equivalent of Kohlberg's "internal dialogue". "Actual dialogue" is meant quite literally. Kohlberg (1981, see Chapter 5) tried to include a process of dialogue in moral-judgment-making through his concept of "moral musical chairs" (i.e., ideal reversible role-taking). Kohlberg's Stage 6 is based on principles of respect for persons that are absolutely compatible with engaging in actual dialogue. The principle of dialogue is included in Kohlberg's (1982) work on moral education within "just communities." In these intervention studies, actual dialogue over moral conflict lasts until a consensus is achieved through the reciprocal alteration of participants' understanding of their own needs.

Kohlberg (1984) was aware of the limitations of internal dialogue (i.e., the "moral musical chairs" activity of prescriptive role-taking), with which "one can only proceed so far intellectually" (p. 386). Stage 6 reasoning, according to Kohlberg, logically necessitates dialogue in actual, real-life moral conflicts. Otherwise, its intent to attain justice could indeed be undermined by self-centered constructions of the needs and outlooks of self and other.

A fourth aspect proposed by Harsanyi (1982), is to reflect on one's choices while realizing one has an equal chance of being in any of those roles implied by the situation in that society. In reply to a moral question, one considers the position of each party involved and then weighs these perspectives according to one's self-chosen ethical principles. Explicit declarations of the intrinsic value, dignity, and equality of every individual in the situation express the attitude of reverence and care for each person as an end in her/himself, not merely as a means toward achieving other ends. Even social welfare or human development must take a back seat to this viewpoint.

The use of universalistic criteria characterizes Stage 6. That is, an actor reflects: "Would I want anyone in my situation not to decide the way I do?" Stage 6 is also characterized by the use of one or more general ethical principles in order to arrive at a fair decision. Such principles are different from either rules or rights; principles tend to apply to all circumstances and are couched in positive prescriptions (e.g., life preservation), rather than negative proscriptions (e.g., don't steal, don't lie, don't kill, don't cheat). At the heart of Stage 6 is a respect for human dignity that may imply sometimes breaking the law or rules or violating societally recognized rights (stealing a drug to save a human life, injecting a lethal dose of morphine at the request of a dying person in pain).

There may be one or several universal principles used in Stage 6 reasoning. Examples include the principle of justice, respect for human individuality or dignity, the principle of maximal utility or benevolence (i.e., act so as to maximize the welfare of all individuals concerned), and the concept of universal human care, or *agape*. There are various principles of justice, including maximizing the quality of life for each person, maximum individual freedom compatible with the equivalent freedom for others, and fairness and equity in distribution of goods and respect. Such moral principles may be espoused either in the language of human rights and duties or in the language of responsibility and care for human "brothers and sisters."

The operations I have been describing are synthesized, at Stage 6, into a totality which establishes a self-reflective structure for ethical decision making. Recall that at Stage 5, law and moral norms are based on the operations of equality, equity, reciprocity, etc. But, according to Stage 6, these operations become self-chosen, self-conscious principles. Given the self-reflection of moral agency and judgment, prescriptive role taking (i.e., balancing perspectives) and universality become functioning principles as well as validity checks on the justifications given for upholding moral laws and norms.

It is accurate to think of Stage 6 as being grounded in the intentional use of the operation of justice as a set of principles to guarantee justice when attempting to resolve moral problems. It is not so much framed on a new understanding beyond the Stage 5 concept of a prior-to-society position: This requires that Stage 6 discourse involve the principle of "moral musical chairs." Consequently, while Stage 5 is supported by an emphasis on fixed contract or agreement, Stage 6 is focused on the process by which agreements or contracts are reached as well as on the guarantees of the fairness of the procedures that underlie such agreement. Beneath the fixed contract and agreement of Stage 5, intended to preserve human rights, is a stress on the salience of protecting human trust and community. Trust and community, at Stage 6, become the premise for dialogue, fairness, human rights, and justice. It is important to note that reasoning at Stage 5 has problems balancing the concept of fixed contract with the underlying notions of trust and community. Stage 6, however, solves this dilemma through the operation of dialogue, a derivative of "moral musical chairs."

Conclusion

It is important that moral theory acknowledge the sociohistorical conditions on which it is based and that define the highest good for the moral actor. Since theory does not exist in a temporal or spatial vacuum, a better grasp of the central issues in moral theory can be gained through the sociology of knowledge.

Cognitive structure and language, which shape our knowledge and moral beliefs, are socially constructed; they are not available prior to experience. This necessitates that we hold off on specifying the basic criteria by which we choose particular value stances as moral. Instead, we view reality in terms of Kant's *phenomena*. Ideas may be regarded as reflections—reflections of their times and cultural settings. Mannheim introduced the concept of "relationism" to address epistemology (as to whether we obtain knowledge through reason, the scientific method, intuition, revelation, and so on) as it relates to the social context. Mannheim's point is central to my thesis that ethnic and cultural factors influence the social and role-taking experiences that shape one's moral development. Relationism was explained by Mannheim by using "constellation" as a metaphor. In addition to the astrological meaning of constellations, dealing with the mutual relationship of the stars and humans, it broadly refers to "the specific combination of certain factors at a given movement. . . . [Thus] the simultaneous presence of various factors is responsible for the shape assumed by that one factor in which we are interested" (Mannheim [1936] 1971: 59).

In the previous chapter, the social context of language and morality was examined. The sociology of knowledge tells us to ask the contextual questions that play just as important a role in guiding theory as issues of epistemology and theoretical content. Consequently, in Chapter 1, I also analyzed the sociohistorical context in which Kohlberg's research evolved. I compared Kohlberg's approach to competing paradigms and argued that specific events that characterized the turbulent and critical 1960s were closely tied to the rise and hegemony of Kohlberg's scientific research program. Political power, economic control, and ultimately, the social fabric of American society were being challenged, giving rise to self-reflection on moral issues. Kohlberg's budding school of moral education questioned mainstream psychology, education, and philosophy; this questioning paralleled the social movements that rebelled against the legitimacy of the status quo. The point is that systems of morality are produced by social, cultural, ethnic, and racial groups who do not live in the isolated shelter of a private existence but rather in a particular historical era and cultural setting. In other words, ethics is a product of human interaction; knowledge is socially constructed.

Kant, Piaget, Kohlberg, and Habermas view society as a total system characterized by the integration and unification of its parts (e.g., belief and value systems). On the other hand, I propose a pluralist perspective on morality. Quite simply, societies consist of divergent groups with varying interests. No ethnic, racial, and cultural groups are identical; they differ in terms of language, status, wealth, power, customs, and tradition. Yet such variance is not necessarily dysfunctional. Moral plurality, clearly, creates dilemmas, but it also encourages openness and change. Moral plurality is both objective and subjective; it reflects vacillating emphases on individual and group rights. It indicates that people are both social and self-interested. Moral plurality demonstrates the high degree of interconnectedness between consciousness, meaning and symbols, and the structures of ethnic, racial, class, and gender inequality.

4

Moral Judgment Method:
Problems and Alternatives

We shall willingly grant that bad faith is a lie to oneself.
—*Jean-Paul Sartre*, Being and Nothingness

If you cannot keep your promise, then you can never be honest
with anybody—not even yourself.
—*Subject number 33 (white female)*

Kohlberg studied moral development for over thirty years. In 1955
he began his dissertation (Kohlberg 1958) at the University of Chicago, expanding the pioneering study by Piaget ([1932] 1965) of the
development of moral judgment in children.

Kohlberg's research has led to the identification of a culturally
invariant sequence of moral stages (Kohlberg 1969). Longitudinal
data (Nisan and Kohlberg, 1982; Kohlberg, 1969; Edwards, 1975;
Colby et al. 1983) have been presented to establish, validly and reli-
ably, the universal and invariant sequence of moral judgment stages.
A research instrument and scoring system that accurately measure
moral judgment in individuals is crucial; if the method is unreliable,
the ability to draw substantial conclusions about the validity of
Kohlberg's theory is critically impaired.

I critique the Standard Issue scoring system in this chapter.
How the current scoring system came to be and why it is worth
examining is shown in a brief discussion of the background of moral
judgment scoring. Standard Issue Scoring is briefly described. After
that, the Moral Judgment Interview is evaluated for ecological validity, how well the research instrument represents real life (e.g., allows a variety of choices and responses and parallels personally

63

experienced and relevant situations). (See Appendix for the Moral Judgment Interview, Form A.) Problems with scoring procedures are considered. Three forms of reliability (test–retest, alternate form, and interrater) used to judge the scoring system, and three types of instrument validity (construct, discriminant, and predictive) are examined. Finally, I briefly discuss some methodological problems with the type of statistical analysis that Kohlberg's research team uses to validate the cognitive development model.

The Background of the Moral Judgment Method

Kohlberg's moral judgment scoring system has been substantially reformulated since his original study (Kohlberg 1958). The early scoring systems—sentence rating and global story rating—were essentially content analyses. They yielded enough anomalies in the analysis of longitudinal data by Kramer (1968) to warrant revision of stage definitions and scoring methods. Specifically, Kramer found numerous cases of individual regression and stage skipping. The revisions provided a clearer differentiation of moral judgment structure from its content.

In 1971, structural issue scoring was constructed by which a "stage was assigned to material within each content unit on the basis of level of perspective" (Colby et al. 1983: 8). Although this scoring system was an improvement over earlier systems, large units of interview material were necessary for scoring. Scoring criteria became general and abstract. Consequently, scoring was subjective and often unreliable (Colby et al. 1983).

The critique by Kurtines and Greif (1974) revealed the need for a reliable scoring instrument. The data did not support the universal applicability of postconventional stages. Test–retest reliability of the scoring procedure also needed to be established. Kurtines and Greif examined the study by Turiel (1966) to evaluate this. In the interval between the pretest and posttest, the dominant stage scores of the control group decreased by 6.1 percent. This change was the largest obtained in the study. Kurtines and Greif contended that pretest–posttest dissimilarity in the control group subjects meant that any change measures were uninterpretable.

Perhaps the most salient criticism of Kohlberg's theory and method is the apparent gap between moral judgment and moral action. Kurtines and Greif charged that the scoring system was deficient in predictive validity. They cited a study by Haan, Smith and Block (1968), where subjects who scored at Stage 2 in fact showed the same behavior as subjects who scored at Stage 6. (The predictive validity of Kohlberg's method will be discussed later.)

Kurtines and Greif applied criteria from standarized testing to judge Kohlberg's data from clinical interviews. Broughton (1975) and Turiel (1978) argue that it is not scientifically legitimate to use standards from one methodology (e.g., psychometric) to evaluate the worth of data generated from another methodology (e.g., clinical). Kurtines and Greif's critique reflects "a common and mistaken attempt to reduce structural development in cognition to static psychometric traits, an attempt which confuses developmental theories with measurement instruments" (Broughton 1975: 81). Kurtines and Greif views the merits of Kohlberg's theory and scoring system as a single issue, not as two separate ones. They called attention to the only minimal changes over time in moral judgment scores. (Turiel 1966; 1969; 1972). Nevertheless, this is consistent with the interactional basis of development.

Piaget ([1932] 1965), Kohlberg (1963), and Turiel (1969) recognize that development through the stages of moral reasoning is gradual, not abrupt. Transitional movement is characterized by gradual shifts in the modal type of an individual's reasoning (see Lerner 1976: 182). The internal consistency of a moral stage takes a remarkably long time to develop (Fischer 1983). A new structure of reasoning surfaces first in some dimensions of an individual's thinking and only gradually generalizes across the moral domain. The trend of such development is toward equilibrium in the organism–environment interaction and toward reciprocity between self and other (Kohlberg et al. 1978.)

A major weakness of research on Kohlberg's theory has been the unavailability of standardized, readily administered measures (Kurtines and Greif 1974; Trainer 1977; Siegal 1980.) This is partially due to the premise that the clinical method is the only possible mode of data collection (Kurtines and Pimm 1983). Although this procedure leads to fruitful data, there are problems with its use (Enright, Franklin, and Manheim 1980): lack of standardization, lack of replicability, difficulties with transcription, interviewer training, and time-consuming and expensive scorer training (Kurtines and Pimm 1983).

Referring to the "judgmental nature of the coding procedures", Kurtines and Greif (1974: 456), equate human judgment with error or bias. But to eliminate judgment from coding procedures implies that judgment must be eliminated from research in general (Broughton 1975: 90).

We no longer have to assume that the "unstandardized" approach works against the discovery of lawful relationships, since Piaget's [clinical] method has led to some of the most replicable results in the field of psychology (Cowan et al. 1969: 272).

In fact, "coding that does not involve judgment is invalid, because it does not bear on the meaning of statements" (Broughton 1975: 90). Turiel concludes that "the type of analysis done by Kurtines and Greif provides no basis for negatively or positively evaluating data generated by the clinical method" (1978: 60). Kohlberg, nevertheless, uses psychometric data analysis (e.g., Colby et al. 1983).

Some theoretical and methodological concerns are unsettled. Kohlberg's "bootstrapping" method is not strictly hypothetical-deductive. Data feedback into theory and method has improved the assessment of moral development. Longitudinal data have been presented to counter criticisms of stage models (e.g., Rest 1979a). Nicolayev and Phillips (1978) regard the readjustment of scoring procedures as an illegitimate technique to obtain the results required by the theoretical assumptions. Kohlberg, however, defends theoretical and methodological revision as "progressive." A key result of such revision has been standard issue scoring (Colby et al. 1987) The scoring method has also been called "standard form scoring" (Kohlberg 1981a).

Standard Issue Scoring

Standard issue scoring aims at greater objectivity and reliability than previous systems by specifying exact stage criteria. Each scored unit is a Criterion Judgment defined by the "intersection of Dilemma x Issue x Norm x Element" (Colby et al. 1983: 11). There are three standard forms (A, B, C) of the moral judgment interview (MJI); each consists of three hypothetical moral dilemmas. The dilemmas present a conflict such that a particular response is clearly not the only conceivable one that is acceptable. The conflict forces a choice between two culturally acceptable but incompatible alternatives. For example, the classic "Heinz Dilemma" sets up opposition between a law or norm and a human need: Should Heinz steal a drug to save his dying wife if the only druggist able to provide to the drug insists on a high price that Heinz cannot afford to pay? The interview typically takes from 60 to 90 minutes (Gibbs, Widaman, and Colby 1982).

Each dilemma focuses on two opposed moral choices, each called an "issue," requiring a choice of action. In the Heinz Dilemma, the issues are preserving a life and upholding the law. Each dilemma is followed by nine to ten standardized probe questions designed to elicit justification, elaboration, and clarification of the subject's moral judgment. The subject's initial decision (in the Heinz Dilemma, whether or not to steal the drug) determines the chosen issue. In justifying that choice, the subject appeals to one or more moral values or norms, which indicate what is important to the subject. The norm is then broken down into its elements. The elements indicate why the norm is important. For example, Heinz should steal the drug (life-preservation issue) because he is her husband (affiliation norm) and is therefore supposed to help her (duty element).

The scorer takes a conceptually coherent element, an Interview Judgment (IJ), from the subject's protocol and attempts to match it with a Criterion Judgment (CJ) in the scoring manual. For greater objectivity and higher reliability, each CJ includes a statement of the underlying stage structure reflected in the criterion judgment (stage structure), detailed criteria for defining a match with the criterion judgment (critical indicators), explanations of distinctions among criterion judgments a scorer is likely to confuse (distinctions—other stages), and several examples of interview material which can be considered to match the CJ (match examples). The scorer must determine whether the IJ embodies the CJ. Matches or "guess scores" determine the issue scores. Typically between one and five matches are assigned to a choice (Colby et al. 1983).

The two basic indices constructed from the Moral Judgment Interview (MJI) are the Global Stage Score (GSS) and the Average Weighted Score (AWS). The GSS uses a 9-point scale, specifying pure (e.g., 5) and transitional (e.g., 3/4) stages. The AWS ranges from 100 (pure Stage 1) to 500 (pure Stage 5). (Stage 6 is not included in the scoring manual.)

The six issue scores (two issues x three dilemmas) are used to construct the individual's GSS and AWS. Data collection requires individual interviewing by experienced interviewers and transcription from interview tapes. Verbatim writing out by the interviewer of responses during the interview is very difficult but marginally acceptable (Gibbs et al. 1982). Until recently, reliable scoring virtually required attending the Center for Moral Education's annual Moral Judgment Scoring Workshop at Harvard. This participation has been criticized as discouraging independent research (Kurtines and Greif 1974). Now that the Center has been dismantled, researchers must rely on the scoring manual.

Standard issue scoring has replaced structural issue scoring for greater standardization and reliability. Gibbs et al. (1982) claim that psychometric validation of standard issue scoring has been accomplished. Data from Kohlberg's 20-year longitudinal study (Colby et al. 1983) support standard issue scoring through high test–retest, alternate form, and interrater reliablity. Moreover, the authors state that the data sustain the stage criteria of invariant sequence and structural wholeness.

Despite advances in the current scoring system, several issues are methodologically problematical. Two major issues relevant to generating the data that Colby et al. (1983) wish to employ for establishing the reliability and validity of their procedure are examined in the next two sections. First, the moral judgment interview is considered as to whether it provides data with sufficient ecological validity, and whether ecological validity is an appropriate criterion. Then the focus shifts to problems with scoring. There are two issues here: questions about the definition of stages which suggest invalid resultant stage scores; and problems with the scoring procedure itself, including guess scores, transpositions, gender bias, and interview administration.

The Moral Judgment Interview

Ecological validity refers to how well the research instrument represents the real world. Ecologically valid moral dilemmas describe (personally experienced) situations of importance and familiarity to most people, giving them response freedom by not requiring either/ or judgments.

Data for Ecological Validity

Kohlberg's moral dilemmas have been criticized for a lack of relevance (Simpson 1974; Yussen 1977; Siegal 1980). The MJI "fails to adequately sample 'moral problems.' There has been little effort . . . to discover the characteristics of dilemmas that people themselves deem important" (Yussen 1977: 162). Siegal states: "Kohlberg's method relies too heavily on responses to moral dilemmas which are outside the subjects' personal experiences" (1980: 294).

Children talk with more detail and reach more complicated solutions to dilemmas in spontaneous everyday interactions, not when formally questioned by researchers (Vygotsy 1935; Piaget [1955] 1966; Issacs 1966). These interactions are phenomena that the child knows and cares about, compared to questions used in cognitive and moral assessments which are hypothetical, arbitrary, and perhaps alien in content. This issue is especially important for culturally diverse subjects. Methodologically, the quest for cognitive assessment devices with validity and reliability across various cultural/ethnic groups has led to repeated reformulations of such tests (Cole et al. 1977). Cross-cultural moral judgment studies must accomodate for the probability that such children know and care less about the contexts of standardized tests than do their White Anglo-Saxon Protestant middle-class counterparts.

Real-life decisions are complex and go beyond questions of justice. Some individuals, viewed as "postconventional" by Kohlberg, are ineffective in real-life moral dilemmas; they are unable to apply abstract ethical principles to personal crises (Gilligan 1982). Kohlberg's dilemmas are unrealistic; they depict situations as having rigid either/or choices and consequences (Cortese 1984a). In the Heinz Dilemma, for example, it is implied that if Heinz does not steal the drug, his wife will die. Some of my subjects rejected both "possible" alternatives (Heinz stealing the drug or letting his wife die) and proposed other solutions to the problem:

> **No. 56:** I can't really believe that Heinz couldn't find some means of getting the money, even if it meant selling his prized possession or taking a second mortgage on the house. If he was desperate enough, if he was sincere enough, there would have to be some way of finding the money.
>
> **No. 69:** I presume he should investigate alternate ways of gaining the money. Stealing is no way to achieve anything. It is always best to gain something in [a] proper manner.
>
> **No. 10:** There's no "undecided" in there?
>
> **No. 46:** I realize his wife is dying but there's something else you can retreat to other than crime and violence.
>
> **No. 49:** There's another way of getting money. Even though he couldn't get it from everyone else, he could get a loan from a bank.
>
> **No. 38:** Heinz is in a rough spot. Maybe what he should do is either pick up another job or go to a bank and try the Red Cross, or go the church, to seek other help.
>
> **No. 22:** He could raise some more money to buy the drug.
>
> **No. 21:** Maybe there would have been other options to get the drug. He could have gone through some authority to force the pharmacist to give it to him for a cheaper price.

No. 39: Surely he could find a way to come up with the money, or go to another dealer. Possibly that drug recipe could be discovered by someone else.

No. 30: There are other ways you could go about it. He could have gone to the bank to get a loan. Or other methods, but actually going to steal the drug, no.

No. 34: There are other means of getting it besides stealing. He could go through negotiations and take the man to court to get the drug.

In sum, although Kohlberg's moral dilemmas portray solutions to moral problems in black and white, some of the subjects saw shades of gray. Clearly, Heinz's not stealing the drug does not necessarily mean his wife will die. A parallel real-life dilemma was the widely publicized Karen Quinlan case. The dilemma there was whether or not to "pull the plug," to remove the life-sustaining apparatus from the comatose Quinlan to let her "die with dignity." Quinlan, however, in fact lived (at least technically) for over 10 years after she was separated from the device.

In defense of Kohlberg, although the either/or element in his dilemmas may be artificial, revised versions of standard stories adapted to make them more suitable to culturally diverse populations provoke fresh reasoning by subjects (e.g., Nisan and Kohlberg 1982). But there is still a problem with testing the "best" judgment or the limits of an individual's moral reasoning through the hypothetical dilemmas. Only if individuals have the chance to demonstrate their full potential, can cognitive ability be accurately measured and appreciated (Damon 1977). If this is not allowed, only an incomplete picture of the individual's moral thought will be revealed. There are, nevertheless, no data that indicate that the moral dilemmas are viewed as unimportant or unfamiliar.

In my own research, I found that some of the standard questions put artificial constraints on responses:

Question: If Heinz doesn't love his wife, should he steal the drug for her?

No. 16: If he didn't love his wife—that shouldn't even enter his mind—stealing the drug for her or not, . . . he wouldn't be trying that hard to get it for her if he didn't love her.

Question: According to you, if he doesn't love her, *should* he steal it?

No. 16: He loves her. That's all there is to it. I mean, period. That he doesn't love her doesn't make any sense to me from my point of view.

Other subjects echo the same thought:

No. 19: If he doesn't love her? I don't see how he could possibly even consider doing it if he didn't.

No. 31: He must love his wife. He must have some attachment if he could care enough to ask the druggist to sell it cheaper. If he didn't love his wife, he wouldn't have bothered to ask. He should go ahead and steal the drug because he must love his wife.

These subjects focused on Heinz's care, responsibility, and love for his wife, not justice or rights, the intended focus of the question.

Ecological Validity as Criterion

Moral judgment research can be judged against three methodological criteria (Edwards 1981): (a) Moral dilemmas must raise issues and examine values relevant to the subject's background. This involves either the adaptation of original dilemmas or the creation of appropriate new dilemmas. (b) Research procedures must elicit the best or most representative reasoning of subjects, for this reason, oral interviews are more desirable than written ones. (Edwards' assertion here is debatable: Although oral responses may indicate better reasoning than written responses, both types ought to be valid in literate cultures). (c) Dilemmas and probing questions must be presented in the subject's primary language. Responses should be scored in that language or translated so as not to distort scoring. These three criteria require thorough knowledge of the subject's background.

Perhaps ecological validity is a debatable criterion for moral judgment research. For example, pure (or purer) dilemmas might be a better test than everyday dilemmas; unexperienced dilemmas might elicit best reasoning where the self's own ordinary experience would tend to elicit lower reasoning. There is, after all, a whole history in psychology of at times using ecologically invalid "stimuli" for specific responses (e.g., nonsense syllables, transpositions, oddity problems with geometric shapes) that presumably many subjects found relatively unimportant, entirely novel, and/or constraining. Perhaps idealized measures are more representative of real behaviors or capacities than measures based on everyday life. But the question is whether the goal is to get directly at a process with the cleanest procedure or instead to simulate the real world. To be sure, a measure is not automatically better because, on its face, it looks more like everyday behavior. But a measure such as Kohlberg's should have some relation, at least a predictive, one to everyday behavior.

Scoring Procedures

Stage Definitions

There are methodological problems related to several of the stages. There is little empirical support for Stage 1 (Siegal 1980: 294). Stage 3 is inadequately defined and difficult to score (Siegal 1980: 291). Stage 4½ is also problematic for scoring: The discovery of several subjects regressing from Stage 4 to Stage 2 (Kohlberg and Kramer 1969) was later reinterpreted, which led to the conceptualization of this new substage of relativistic skepticism and meta-ethical reasoning. "At stage 4½, a choice is personal and subjective. It is based on emotions; conscience is seen as arbitrary and relative, as are ideas such as 'duty' and 'morally right' " (Kohlberg 1981b: 411). However, only one of the anomalous cases in the original analysis can be attributed to Stage 4½ (Colby et al. 1983). The whole notion of a relativistic crisis of transition at Stage 4½ is an open question. The problem with scoring subjects at Stage 4½ is that their normative judgments are so similar to those of subjects at lower stages; their protocols do not receive scores of 4½ by standard issue scoring, as might be expected. Instead, subjects are sometimes scored at Stage 2. Poor probing during the original interview permitted confusion of superficial content with deeper forms of reasoning (Broughton 1975).

Scoring Procedures and Problems

In addition to problems with stage definitions, there are deficiencies in the scoring system itself. Guess scores present a potential scoring problem. A guess score is assigned when a protocol yields no clear or marginal match for the issue being scored. If any moral judgment material is available on the issue in question, the scorer must assign a guess score, no matter how nebulous that material might be (Colby et al. 1987).

Insufficient material for match scoring issues can result from deficiencies either in a particular interview or in standard issue scoring. The first situation involves poor probing by the interviewer or resistance or poor elaboration by the subject. Alternatively, sometimes a subject's response may simply not match a CJ in the scoring manual. This is a serious but perhaps unavoidable problem with standard issue scoring, because a subject's thought, though structurally scorable and fully elaborated, may be original or idiosyncratic (Colby et al. 1987). The CJs were empirically generated and are not exhaustive of all possible CJs at each stage.

Standard issue scoring is in fact somewhat of a misnomer: It is not standard at all. The codification of all possible types of response (all conceivable Dilemma x Issue x Norm x Element combinations) is necessary if true standardized scoring is to be attained. This would involve 9 dilemmas x 18 issues x 9 norms x 17 elements = 23,786 combinations of stage-scorable responses! The use of guess scores is an attempt to compensate for a lack of clearly defined criteria for scorable material. A guess score reflects the scorer's best appraisal of the stage suggested by all the material on a particular issue. Such estimates are predicated on the scorer's basic knowledge of the stages.

Transposition by the scorer could also cause reliability problems. This involves the scorer restating interview material more coherently than the subject's expression of it (Colby et al. 1987). Subjects do not always express themselves clearly. Often they begin a thought, interrupt it by commenting on other ideas, and eventually return to their original point. The rater must reconstruct meaning out of misstated words, incomplete phrases, and fragmented sentences. The danger with such reclassification is obvious. A scorer's misinterpretation of interview material can result in substantive changes in the IJ, which could affect stage scoring. The rater could err by either inserting extraneous concepts into the subject's response, i.e., "putting words in the subject's mouth," or by deleting germaine material in the reconstruction process. The comments on guess scoring and transposition are not meant as an attack on scorers' individual interpretation in scoring moral stages. Instead, they point to areas where subjective decisions of raters could result in unreliable issue scores.

Scoring criteria require that interview material be at least implicitly prescriptive (expressed in "should" or "ought" form), justified by reasons given for choice, and viewed as valid by the subject through commitment to choice. There is, however, no control in the scoring system for socially acceptable responses. The sincerity of the subject is always assumed unless explicitly denied by the subject. Moreover, scoring procedures require that only two of six possible issue scores (excluding guess scores) are needed to compute GSSs and AWSs, which means that in the absence of scorable material for as many as two of three dilemmas, GSSs and AWSs can still be assigned. This policy is too lax for a valid assessment of moral development, particularly if stage mixture is evident.

The scoring system has also been criticized for gender bias (Haan, 1975; Holstein, 1976; Gilligan, 1982). Gilligan states that women are generally different from men in their fundamental orientations to life. Distinct masculine and feminine orientations are established early and irrevocably in the mother-child relationship (Chodorow 1978). Given the near pancultural gender role of childrearing for women, boys develop self-identification by contrasting self and mother. Girls, on the other hand, develop self-identification by synthesizing an affinity between self and mother. The contrast between the male child and the other-sex parent against the likeness between the female child and the same-sex parent are then applied to significant others, and eventually, to a generalized other (i.e., Mead 1934).

Gilligan maintains that the feminine orientation is ignored by Kohlberg's theory and methodology. It follows from Chodorow's analysis that men focus on separateness, women on connectedness. Consequently, for men, socialization necessitates a complex moral system of rights and rules of justice. Because of a fundamental separateness, a system of rights is necessary to connect people.

The hypothetical dilemmas focus on principles and the conflict of rights. Women, however, stress concern and responsibility for others and for how one's judgment and behavior affect interpersonal relationships, for example, helping others when one can (Gilligan 1982), not principles and conflict of rights. Kohlberg's scoring system is keyed to abstract modes of response, not a failure of response. The theory of moral development concerns the capacity for making increasingly more sophisticated moral judgments. Regrettably, females were excluded from Kohlberg's original (1958) sample from which his theoretical framework is derived.

The care orientation is expressed continuously by a woman in the following passages:

Question: Suppose the person dying is not his wife but a stranger. Should Heinz steal the drug for a stranger?

No. 16: No. If the guy's a stranger, he probably doesn't care about the guy enough. There are other people who care about the guy. Whoever cares about the guy is going to get it for him one way or another.

Question: Is it important for people to do everything they can to save another's life?

A.: Yeah. It's just human to care about another person.

Q.: It is against the law for Heinz to steal. Does that make it morally wrong?

A.: No. Because when there's love in your heart it doesn't matter. You shouldn't care what somebody else is gonna do to you. The price you have to pay later isn't really important, at the time, for what you have to do now.

Q.: Should people try to do everything they can to obey the law?

A.: Yeah, but this is beyond obeying the law. That's the only way he can get it. He can't do anything else besides steal it to get the drug. Law comes second after caring.

Q.: Should Officer Brown report Heinz for stealing?

A.: No. Because he does know the situation. If he knows Heinz, he knows that Heinz needs it for his wife. And that again is a matter of caring. If he's a friend of Heinz, he won't report it.

Q.: How does [punishing people who break the law] apply to how the Judge should decide?

A.: No matter how smart you are, you still have to have some feelings for people. And, hopefully, he will have feelings for Heinz.

The care orientation is contextual, personal, and centered on responsibility to significant others; the justice orientation is abstract, positional, or hierarchical, and centered on the rights of the generalized other. Yet the responsibility orientation is a dimension of morality not usually tapped through Standard Issue Scoring:

Question: What do you think is the most important thing a son should be concerned about in his relationship to his father?

No. 58: Care for each other.

Question: Thinking in terms of society, should people who break the law be punished?

No. 3: Each case has to be looked at separately. You can't help but feel compassion in some cases. Human compassion is a very necessary thing when you're deciding on a person.

Question: How does this apply to how the judge should decide?

No. 14: Heinz was involved in a situation where his wife was dying. He was not thinking of whether it was right or wrong. He was thinking of the care of his wife.

Women view the failure of the druggist to demonstrate responsibility to his fellow human beings as the crux of the Heinz dilemma:

No. 7: The druggist is wrong in trying to make a profit off of dying people.

No. 8: I think his behavior could be looked at as sort of selfish. Even though it's not socially sanctioned to steal it, I think that it's morally okay under the circumstances.

No. 19: What the druggist is doing is morally wrong. He's basically trying to steal from other people. The druggist is not breaking any laws, but in a way he's breaking a law of humanity.

No. 17: If [Heinz] thinks that the druggist is charging too much, he can work through the court system. Of course, it may be too late for his wife, but he may be able to help someone else, if what the pharmacist is doing is illegal. I don't know if it is illegal to make a profit. It should be.

No. 14: If the drug only costs $200 and he's charging $2,000 I think that's outrageous. A person's life is far more important than the money involved.

No. 53: The druggist was very selfish.

No. 32: The law should intervene because the druggist is wrong for charging such an exorbitant price for that radium.

No. 5: It's a matter of life, and the druggist is not budging and is being unreasonable for what he is asking for the drug. He's evaluating the money and not the human life. Heinz did it for his wife and went against this corrupt druggist who wanted to make a lot of money.

No. 42: The druggist is cheating Heinz, whose wife is dying.

No. 65: A human should always help another human and the chemist is being unfair.

No. 56: The druggist is selling the drug at an exorbitant price. Everything he is doing is morally wrong.

No. 16: The druggist is not going to help at all. He shouldn't have to make that much money. And he should understand. A druggist is there to supply medicine to people who need it; and he's not doing it.

These women solved problems through relationships, interdependence, and connection with other people, not abstract moral principles. In response to the question: Should Heinz steal the drug?, the women focused on the word "steal." But the question is intended to be answered by focusing on the word "should." That is what makes it a question of justice. Thus, the women are actually answering a different question. They see Heinz as already involved and having a responsibility to act. For Kohlberg, the question is whether to act; for these women, the moral dilemma is how to act.

Women view the dilemma as a communication problem. Heinz needs to communicate with the druggist, his own friends, the bank, the police, or whomever else can help to resolve the problem. Once there is adequate communication, the solution is set. The salience of communication emerges clearly in the following interview segment:

> **Question:** What do you think is the most important thing a son should be concerned about in his relationship to his father?
>
> **No. 38:** The communication between him and his father.
>
> **Q.:** Why is that the most important thing?
>
> **A.:** Because in order to really know what's going on with each other you need communication. If there is no communication, then you really don't know what is happening one way or the other.
>
> **Q.:** What do you think is the most important thing a father should be concerned about in his relationship to his son?
>
> **A.: It's also communication.**
>
> **Q.:** Why is that the most important thing?
>
> **A.:** Because again for the father to teach the son anything or to learn anything from his son, they have to communicate. If they don't communicate, then there is no exchange of information.

The responsibility and justice orientations to morality are thematic, not gender differences. A person of either gender, could have either or both orientations. Both are important for moral reasoning. It is questionable whether "formal structures represent a sufficient and comprehensive array of those moral levels that people actually use" (Haan 1978: 302).

Interpersonal morality depicts the basic way in which people relate to themselves, others, and their society. This morality transpires from dialogue between actors who achieve symmetrical accord based on give-and-take and shared interests. Formal morality transpires from individual tendencies. "The moral reasoning of males who live in technical, rationalized societies, who reason at the level of formal operations and who defensively intellectualize and deny interpersonal and situational detail" (Haan 1978: 287) is favored in Kohlberg's model. Future research should transcend scoring systems which tap only formal morality. There is a need for a multi-dimensional model that incorporates interpersonal and subcultural morality and moral action.

Colby and Damon (1983) state that Gilligan's data do not support a thesis of gender bias in Kohlberg's theory. They indicate that evidence in support of Gilligan's distinction between gender orientations is mixed: "The available research data . . . do not reveal a clear picture of a global dichotomy between the life orientations of men and women" (1983: 476). Women seem to pass through the same invariant sequence of moral stages as men. Colby and Damon argue that Kohlberg's scoring system cannot be accused of gender bias unless women score lower than men. Kohlberg's theory allows for people's progressing at varying rates and fixating at different end points of development because of role-taking and decision-making opportunities. Thus, women could score lower than men without this directly discrediting Kohlberg's theory or method. Recent literature reviews (Rest 1983; Walker 1984) reveal that when education and occupation of subjects are controlled, there are no significant gender differences in moral development.

A final point on the scoring procedure concerns the administration of the moral judgment interview. A subject may score either higher or lower than first evaluated by elaborating on a point. After a scorable Interview Judgment has been obtained, a probe may stimulate a further response, or unsolicited elaboration by the subject may occur which alters the level of the subject's original IJ. Differential probing by interviewers affects a subject's elaboration, so varying interviewing styles can affect a subject's GSS and AWS.

Reliability

Reliability refers to the degree to which various operations of the same concept yield the same results, i.e., the degree to which observations of a study are repeatable (Bohrnstedt and Knoke 1982). Reliability also points to the degree to which scores on a measure are consistent and unaffected by random error (Stang and Wrightsman 1981). One source of random error for the MJI may be interviewing style. Kohlberg's scoring procedure has been criticized for its lack of reliability and validity (Kurtines and Greif 1974; Yussen 1977), which has prompted the construction of procedures for standardizing moral assessment (e.g. Rest 1979b, Enright et al. 1980). Such standard assessments measure comprehension of and preferences in already posed moral judgments; conversely, standard issue scoring measures spontaneous moral judgments in reply to open-ended questions.

The reliability of standard issue scoring will be reviewed according to test–retest, alternative form, and interrater reliability. Test–retest reliability is the correlation between identical measures administered at different times (Stang and Wrightsman 1981). Colby et al. (1983) administered test–retest MJIs with 43 subjects using Form A, 31 subjects using Form B, and 10 subjects using both A and B. Intervals between Time 1 and Time 2 spanned 3 to 6 weeks, with testing situations held stable. Subjects ages ranged from 8 to 28; gender was nearly evenly distributed. Test–retest reliability correlations for Forms A and B are both in the high 90s. (No test–retest data for Form C were reported by Colby et al.) Virtually all subjects in their retest scored within one-half of a stage of their original test (e.g., from 3 to ¾). Nearly 75 percent of the subjects received the same GSSs on A and B. Those subjects whose scores changed were as likely to score lower as higher on the retest. The researchers view this finding as an indication that changes cannot be attributed to the effect of practicing. Finally, no age nor gender differences were found in test–retest reliability.

Alternate or parallel form reliability is the correlation between similar but not identical measures administered at different times (Stang and Wrightsman 1981). Alternative form data between Forms A and B are based on the test–retest subjects (n = 10 for A and B) and 223 longitudinal MJIs. One scorer rated both forms of the test–retest sample MJIs. All MJIs were scored within one-third of a stage of each other for the two forms; 75 percent received identical scores for A and B. The correlation between AWSs for Forms A and B in this sample was .95. Correlations between A and B using the longitudinal data are not as high, at .84. Since each form was scored by a different rater, reliability coefficients confound form and rater differences. Reliability between Form C and Forms A (.82) and B (.84) also confound form and rater differences.

Interrater reliability is the extent to which two or more scorers record identical observations of the same event (Stang and Wrightsman 1981). In standard issue scoring, this refers to interrater agreement in coding a subject's response (e.g., Is IJ X an example of CJ X, or not?). Test–retest data were also used to examine interrater reliability. Form A MJIs (n = 20) were rated independently by 5 scorers; Form B MJIs (n = 10) were scored by 4 raters; Form C (MJIs (n = 20) were scored independently by 2 raters. Absolute percentage figures for interrater reliability on Form A ranged from 88 percent to 100 percent for agreement within a third of a stage, and from 75 percent to 88 percent for complete agreement (based on the 9-point scale). The correlations for scorers 1 and 2 on MJIs were reported at .98 (Form A), .96 (Form B), and .92 (Form C). Raters varied in degree of scoring experience, although reliability coefficients between the less experienced and more experienced were as high as reliability among the experienced raters. Generally, inter-rater reliability coefficients resemble test–retest coefficients. Although correlations are in the 90s, it should be noted that the scorers in the study included the scoring manual authors. Moreover, recall that the sample was heterogeneous in age; the correlations may have been inflated by the age covariation (Gibbs et al. 1982).

Validity

Validity refers to the degree to which a noted score mirrors an authentic score, undisturbed by systematic error or random error (Stang and Wrightsman 1981). A test or procedure is valid if it measures what it is trusted to measure. Three types of validity are examined here: construct, discriminant, and predictive validity.

Construct validity, the most significant kind of test validity, measures the extent to which the fundamental structures or constructs that the instrument is believed to measure do in fact explain a subject's efficiency on the test (Cook and Campbell 1979). This type of validity is most sharply linked to theory:

> For a measure of moral judgment stage, the two most critical empirical criteria of construct validity correspond to the two most central theoretical assumptions of the stage construct . . . invariance of stage sequence and "structural wholeness" or internal consistency (generality of stage usage across moral issues or dilemmas). (Colby et al. 1983: 26)

Colby and her associates interpret their results to support a stage theory of development and the validity and reliability of the scoring method.

> Our subjects did seem to use a coherent structural orientation in thinking about a variety of moral dilemmas. Their thinking developed in a regular way up the stage sequence, neither skipping stages nor reverting to use of a prior stage. Our results also serve

to validate the moral judgment stages as operationally defined in Standard Form Scoring and to indicate that the Standard Form is a reliable and valid measure of moral judgment. (1983: 76)

With few exceptions, attributed to scoring error, the subjects of the study by Colby and the others (1983) proceeded through the stages in the prescribed order.

What types of change could be permitted under the invariant sequence hypothesis?

> A pattern of no change would not be disconfirming, as moral de-velopment is not hypothesized to occur at any specific rate. Nei-ther would a pattern of progress from one stage to a stage two higher in the alleged sequence be disconfirming, since the individ-ual may have passed through the intervening stage during the in-terval between testings. The only disconfirming pattern, then, is regression to a lower stage. . . . It clearly becomes the case, then, that [Kohlberg's] data . . . occupy a very weak empirical status: They are not capable of disconfirming the hypothesis. (Kuhn 1976: 163–164)

Stage skipping is a metaphysical condition that can never be disproved. Negation of the claim would require proof that a partic-ular stage had never been displayed by an individual. Only two cases from Kohlberg's longitudinal data had more than a one-stage advance in the interval between testings (Broughton 1975: 85). The possibility of skipping stages is not empirical, thus precluding proof. Kuhn found that progressive and regressive changes were equally likely over 6-month intervals. In the course of one-year in-tervals, however, significant progressive change was found.

A high degree of internal consistency in assigned stage scores is suggested by the assumption that stages form "structured wholes" (Colby et al. 1983). One measurement of internal consistency in moral judgment is the proportion of each subject's judgments scored at each stage. Colby et al. (1983) discovered that the great majority of their interviews were scored at either one moral judg-ment stage or two adjacent stages. The overall average percentage of moral judgments at the subject's modal stage was 67 percent. The overall mean percentage of judgments at the individual's two most frequent stages (always adjacent) was 99 percent. If a protocol received 10 percent or less of its scores at any particular stage, this can be treated as scoring error (Colby et al. 1987), and overlooked.

Although the data on internal consistency are impressive, nevertheless, some subjects exhibited judgments from three stages, necessitating the establishment of a limit to this error procedure. The established 10 percent error limit is not enforced in assigning GSSs; a stage must receive at least 25 percent of the total assigned points to be entered as a minor stage. This policy thus overstates the internal consistency of the instrument by disregarding inconsistent stages not counted as scoring error. In other words, if a subject uses a particular stage 10 percent (or less) of the time, it is considered to be the result of scoring error and is consequently ignored in assigning a GSS. If a subject uses a second stage at least 25 percent of the time, it is accommodated into the subject's GSS as a minor stage. But it is hypothetically possible for a subject to use a particular stage between 10 and 25 percent of the time. This is not accounted for in the scoring manual. It represents the range between scoring error and minor stage.

Standard issue scoring has been devised to maximize internal consistency; inconsistent moral dilemmas and scoring techniques have been purged (Rest 1983). How does the internal consistency of the MJI compare to other methods? Gibbs et al. (1982) reported that their subjects' use of a modal stage in a sample that was used to construct the sociomoral reflection measure (SRM), a group administered version of Kohlberg's MJI, was 65 percent; for a second sample, the reliability of the method was 58 percent. Corresponding percentages for the MJI are in the low 70s and high 60s (Colby et al. 1983). For the defining issues test (DIT), an objective measure of moral preference, none of the stage scores have an internal consistency reliability above 60 percent (Davison 1979). In sum, other measures have indicated lower internal consistency in moral judgment than the MJI.

There is one point regarding the internal consistency of moral reasoning that has not been of major concern to researchers. There is not much variation in moral stage among the subjects in the Colby et al. (1983) study. Stage 3 seems to be very prominent in the scoring (Colby et al. 1983: 29–34, Table 13). Indeed, Stages 2 and 3 (and to a lesser extent Stage 4) dominate for most of the 20-year period studied. If subjects fit into only a few categories, then it is hardly surprising that those categories predominate in their protocols. For example, if subjects' behavior almost always fits categories A or B, then—whatever the base rates of A and B—it could be expected that randomly most subjects would show consistency, producing more than 50 percent of either A or B. With any system that effectively discriminates only a small number of categories, "consistency" will be artificially elevated in this way.

Discriminant validity is established if low correlations are found between one method of measuring a construct and a similar method of measuring other unconnected constructs (Campbell and Fiske 1959). When two constructs that are theoretically unassociated prove indeed to be empirically unrelated, discriminant validity is supported. Kohlberg's method has been criticized for not being independent of other correlates (Kurtines and Greif 1974). Colby et al. (1983) do not present evidence for the discriminant validity of standard issue scoring. Rather, they call for further longitudinal research on discriminant and construct validity, specifically with culturally diverse subjects. The key question seems to be: Is there a basis for believing that the constructs measured should be able to be discriminated from moral judgment, or should these constructs be correlated with it? Also, of course, there can be a modest correlation with still strong discriminant validity, so long as the variables can be shown to be measuring different (yet correlated) constructs.

Predictive validity refers to how well scale scores predict, that is, highly correlate with, behavior under specific conditions (Stang and Wrightsman 1981). As noted previously, Kurtines and Greif viewed the predictive validity of Kohlberg's method as minimal. The reply by Broughton (1975) to Kurtines and Greif mentions several studies (Krebs 1967; Kohlberg, 1969 1970; Milgram 1974; Gunzberger, Wegner, and Anooshian 1977; Krebs and Rosenwald 1977) that provide evidence of the relation of moral judgment to action. Nevertheless, while such evidence is clearly supportive, it is by no means conclusive. The low predictive validity of Kohlberg's method is the major criticism of Kurtines and Greif that seems to remain unrefuted. The longitudinal data of Colby et al. (1983) do not provide evidence for predictive validity. They raise the question of whether the recently developed substage construct might prove to be at least as good a predictor of moral action as the moral judgment stage. Kohlberg viewed the lack of predictive validity as a serious problem (Dan Candee, personal communication, June 19, 1981); research is being conducted and encouraged to address this unsettled question (Kohlberg and Candee 1984).

There is considerable support for the hypothesis that moral reasoning and moral action are statistically related (Blasi 1980). However, the degree of support varies from area to area. For example, it is strongest for the hypothesis which suggests moral reasoning differences between delinquents and non-delinquents. But there is minimal support for the notion that postconventional individuals resist more than others the social pressures to conformity in their moral action. There appears to be a lack of integrated and theoretically lucid justifications for formulating some of the particular relationships. Problems of methodological inadequacy and sample selection are typical in moral action studies. At times, positive correlations have been found between moral judgment and certain behaviors that do not seem to be specifically moral. The processes that relate judgment to action need to be identified. For example, what leads individuals from judgment to action? This issue involves the relation between affect and cognition, an important but underemphasized area in previous research.

Statistical Analysis

There appear to be increasing doubts about the adequacy of the type of statistical analysis that Kohlberg employed to validate his theory. According to the assumption of structural wholeness (see Cortese 1987), "moral judgment development is a single general domain cutting across verbal dilemmas and issues" (Colby et al. 1983: 37). Colby et al. (1983) used a factor analysis to test this hypothesis.

"Factor analysis refers to a variety of statistical techniques whose common objective is to represent a set of variables in terms of a smaller number of hypothetical variables." (Kim and Mueller 1978: 9). The Moral Judgment Interview, for example, samples the moral reasoning of individuals across, methodologically speaking, a wide range of dilemmas, issues, and norms. Individual responses to questions from the Moral Judgment Interview then constitute observed variables.

The first step of the analysis generally involves an examination of the interrelationships among these variables. One could use the correlation coefficient as a measure of association and construct a table of correlations. Inspection of the correlation matrix may show that here are positive relationships among these variables (i.e., replies to questions from the Moral Judgment Interview), and that the relationships within some subsets of variables are higher than those between the subsets. A factor analysis may then be used to address whether these moral judgments can be explained by the existence of a small number of hypothetical variables.

A researcher may not know how many underlying dimensions there actually are for the specified data. Consequently, factor analysis may be used as tactical means of discovering the minimum number of hypothetical factors that can explain the marked covariation, and as a way of investigating the data for conceivable data deduction. This type of factor analysis is *exploratory*.

But the use of factor analysis need not be restricted to checking the underlying dimensions of the data. The method may also be used to examine particular hypotheses. For example, Kohlberg (1969) has proposed that there is only one underlying dimension to moral reasoning. If factor analysis is used to test this hypothesis, then it is used as a way of confirming a specific theory. Therefore, it is called *confirmatory* factor analysis.

Recall that according to cognitive-development theory, stages form "structured wholes." Given the assumption of structural wholeness, there should be a high degree of internal consistency in the assignment of individuals' stage scores. Kohlberg and Colby (1983) have interpreted structural wholeness as the use of two adjacent stages. Colby et al.'s (1983) 20-year longitudinal study of moral development sought to document the fundamental assumptions of Kohlberg's theory. Their findings exhibited a high degree of internal consistency in stage scores assigned with virtually all of the interviews receiving scores at two adjacent stages.

They further studied this hypothesis with a principal components analysis. Principal components are:

> linear combinations of observed variables, possessing properties such as being orthogonal to each other, and the first principal component representing the largest amount of variance in the data, the second representing the second largest and so on; often considered variants of common factors, but more accurately they are contrasted with common factors which are hypothetical (Kim and Mueller 1978: 78).

Each of the dilemmas to which subjects replied in the research were scored for six different moral issues (Life, Law, Conscience, Punishment, Contract, and Authority). Colby et al. factor analyzed the correlations among stage scores on each of these issues across dilemmas. In each case, the eigenvalue and corresponding proportion of variance accounted for by the first factor far exceeded those of succeeding factors. An eigenvalue is a mathematical property of a matrix; it is "used in relation to the decomposition of a covariance matrix, both as a criterion of determining the number of factors to extract and a measure of variance accounted for by a given dimension" (Kim and Mueller 1978: 76).

Only one interpretable factor emerged from Colby et al.'s (1983) data even when the multiple factors were subjected to orthogonal and oblique rotations. Orthogonal rotation is "the operation through which a simple structure is sought under the restriction that factors be orthogonal (or uncorrelated); factors obtained by this method are by definition uncorrelated" (Kim and Mueller 1978: 78). Oblique rotation is "the operation through which a simple structure is sought; factors are rotated without imposing the orthogonality condition and resulting terminal factors are in general correlated with each other" (Kim and Mueller, 1978: 78).

Colby et al. (1983) interpreted their results to support the structural wholeness assumption. They inferred that moral judgment is a single, basic domain. But there is a deficiency in their examination. Principal components analysis is not the suitable method (Cortese 1989a).

Stages form a series of qualitative transformations in the nature of an individual's thought. Cognitive development tests should disclose a distinct complexity when student or adult populations are distributed across different cognitive stages (William Rau, personal communication, January 21, 1985). As a result, intercorrelations of cognitive development tests should be much "weaker" than intercorrelations of structural relations within and between measurement sets (e.g., individual differences on composite IQ scales). There will be smaller correlations, and greater variance among correlations. They should reflect a pronounced nonlinear gradient.

Conventional factor analysis splits variables across a number of different factors, since data have multivariate normal distribution. Data must take this distributional form for conventional factor analysis to accurately write them onto a set of metric coordinates or factors. Theoretically, one can hypothesize that tests of moral development will be strongly nonlinear. Factor analysis, however, is a statistical technique that obfuscates the pattern specified in Kohlberg's theory (see Cortese 1989a). Given the original hypothesis of structural wholeness by Kohlberg, writing correlations onto a set of metric coordinates or factors and then comparing factor loadings simply makes no sense.

Rather, Kohlberg's theory points to the use of a common factor procedure. A common factor is an "unmeasured (or hypothetical) underlying variable which is the source of variation in at least two observed variables under consideration" (Kim and Mueller 1978: 76). Common factor procedures include principal axis factoring and a maximum likelihood solution. Principal axis factoring is "a method of initial factoring in which the adjusted correlation matrix is decomposed hierarchically; a principal axis factor analysis with iterated communalities lead to a least-squares solution of initial factoring" (Kim and Mueller 1978: 78). A least-squares solution generally minimizes the squared deviations between the observed values and predicted values. It is a method of extracting initial factors, whose variants include principal axis factoring with iterated communalities. A maximum likelihood solution, in general, is:

> a method of statistical estimation which seeks to identify the population parameters with a maximum likelihood of generating the observed sample distribution; a method of obtaining the initial factor solution; its variants include canonical factoring (RAO) and a method that maximizes the determinant of the residual partial correlation matrix (Kim and Mueller 1978: 78).

In addition to the unsuitability of principal components analysis, a confirmatory rather than exploratory factor analysis procedure should be used to test Kohlberg's theory since the issue involves confirming a hypothesis, not exploring underlying dimensions. A maximum likelihood procedure such as LISREL (Joreskog and Sorbom 1983) has the advantage of providing an analytical, direct test of whether one (or more) factors account for the covariation among the six issue scores.

I (Cortese 1989a) inspected whether a single underlying factor is sufficient to account for between issue correlations in moral stage scores. "Perhaps Kohlberg's homogeneous sample contributed to the high degree of internal consistency in moral reasoning" (Cortese 1989a: 279). Considering Kohlberg's claim that moral stages are culturally universal, structural wholeness should also exist in the moral judgments of women and in culturally diverse populations. Consequently, my (Cortese 1989a) sample was evenly divided between gender and three racial/ethnic categories. Given the improperness of principal components analysis for testing structural wholeness, principal axis factor analysis and LISREL were used. I also reanalyzed Colby et al.'s (1983) data with these same methods. The results of principal axis factor analyses and LISREL in my (Cortese 1989a) sample and in a reanalysis of Colby et al.'s (1983) data indicated that a single underlying factor was adequate to account for between issue correlations in moral stage scores. Even in a sample evenly apportioned by gender and three racial/ethnic categories, fundamentally the same rate of internal consistency was evident as was detected by Colby et al. (1983).

My (Cortese 1989a) study presented several increments to Colby et al. (1983)—it analyzed a data set that was in some ways more diverse; it included women and ethnic/racial minorities and it applied a more elaborate methodology. Nevertheless, although my (1989a) sample may not have been homogeneous with respect to gender and ethnic background, it contained only college students and was more homogeneous than the Colby et al. (1983) sample with respect to age, education level, and possibly social background. The significance of my (1989a) findings is that they further supported Kohlberg's theory and measure of moral judgment, especially for women and ethnic/racial minorities. The evidence can be viewed as consistent with the structural wholeness hypothesis and a step toward validating it, but in itself not an irrefutable proof of the hypothesis.

Conclusion

Moral development remains one of the least understood aspects of comparative human development. This deficiency is the result of difficulties in measuring moral judgment. The cognitive development approach to morality can be characterized as a search for stages of reasoning which have structure and sequence. Kohlberg's research over the past 25 years has focused on establishing the validity and reliability of his model and method. Kohlberg's current research procedure, standard issue scoring, is evaluated in this chapter.

The MJI has been criticized for a lack of relevance. Kohlberg's moral dilemmas present their alternative solutions as black and white rather than as shades of grey. Abstract moral principles which as Gilligan (1982) posits, may not apply to multidimensional, personal crises, are emphasized in Kohlberg's scoring procedures. Yet despite the either/or format, there are no data that indicate that subjects consider the moral dilemmas as unimportant and unfamiliar. However, it should not be assumed automatically that ecological validity alone is an appropriate criterion for moral judgment methodology.

Current scoring procedures were critiqued in this chapter. There are methodological problems related to definitions of several stages. Standard issue scoring is not really standardized. The assignment of guess scores and the transposition of interview material are two areas where the judgment of scorers could result in reliability problems. The codification of many more types of responses is necessary if the standardization of the scoring system is to be achieved.

There is no procedure for checking whether a subject is supplying straightforward responses to dilemma questions. Rest (1979b) provides tests for a subject's honesty through the use of "M" (meaningless) statements in the DIT. Moreover, standard issue scoring appears too lenient by requiring only two of six possible issue scores to calculate GSSs and AWSs. In other words, scorable material is required for only one of three dilemmas in the Moral Judgment Interview. Although a gender bias in Kohlberg's theory and method is suggested by Gilligan (1982), the literature is generally void of studies which point to sex differences in moral judgment. Nevertheless, an allocentric cognitive style, characteristic of white male reasoning, seems to be particularly valued in standard issue scoring.

In the test–retest reliability study by Colby et al. (1983), subjects whose scores changed were as likely to score lower as higher on the posttest. Concerning construct validity, non-modal, inconsistent stage usage unaccounted for by scoring error (10%) is disregarded in standard issue scoring. The scoring procedure should be expanded to include stage usage that represents the range between error and minor stage (i.e., 11–24% of the total stage scores observed).

Clearly, the current scoring procedures successfully answer the major problems with reliability raised by Kurtines and Greif (1974). But the invariant sequence of Kohlberg's highest moral stages has yet to be demonstrated. Moreover, the paradox of validating stage skipping also poses problems for the assumption of invariant stage sequence. There does not seem to be strong evidence for the discriminant or predictive validity of standard issue scoring. But possibly the most serious flow in standard issue scoring is the apparent gap between moral judgment and moral action. Although the assumptions of cognitive development theory center on meaning rather than behavior, the distance between moral judgment and action must be reduced if predictive validity is to be attained.

Standard issue scoring is supported by numerous types of data. Yet validity and reliability problems remain. Longitudinal research is necessary to establish the invariant sequence of postconventional moral stages. There is also a need for longitundinal data from Third World cultures to examine the construct and discriminant validity of standard issue scoring. Comparative research is important for assessing the validity of cognitive development theory and exploring antecendent conditions for moral development. Gender appears to be a key variable for future cultural research. Such investigation may provide the data that undoubtedly will lead to further revision of theory and method and better insight into moral development.

5

Ethnicity And Critique
Of Moral Theory

A dog teaches a boy fidelity.

—*Robert Benchley*

Question: Would you steal for your pet?
Answer: If the pet were the only friend I had.

—*Subject Number 48 (Chicano male)*

This chapter focuses on the effect of ethnicity and social class on human development; it highlights how modes of moral judgment differ according to cultural and subcultural backgrounds. In addition, the cognitive development model of moral reasoning is critically evaluated. Data used to support the cultural universality of moral stages are questioned. Of particular interest, the cognitive development model presupposes primacy of reversibility—taking the position of the others—in moral judgment structures' concept of justice. Moral principles that are allegedly universal are viewed as the highest good. But one may take the position that people are more important than principles, that relationships are more crucial than conceptions of justice, and that subcultural moral systems are more relevant than universal standards of ethics.

Kohlberg assumed that everyone will progress through the same sequence of moral stages regardless of culture, race, ethnicity, social class, or gender. However, this chapter will maintain that the cultural context of moral judgment must be taken into account. A critique of research used to support the validity of Kohlberg's theory challenges the claim that moral stages are universal. Gilligan's and my own research findings will also be discussed, which point

91

to gender, ethnic and racial differences in moral styles. In conclusion, I argue for for a pluralistic theory of moral development. The chapter begins with an examination of how ethnicity and social class affect human development in individuals.

Ethnic Background and Social Class

Human social and cognitive development is largely an outcome of the child-rearing practices of the cultural subgroups that make up a modern complex society (Havighurst 1976: 56). Ethnic groups are people who have a common history and generally shared ways of life, including language, religion, and social identity. They influence their individuals through family activity, peer group, linguistic concepts, common literature, work in formal associations, in-group marriage, and residential and work segregation. Social classes, too, are pervasive and powerful in their influence on individuals (Gordon 1964: 52; Havighurst 1976: 56). Ethnic groups, however, are also effective, more so at the lower and working-class levels than at the middle- and upper-middle-class levels.

There has been a recent controversy over the relative significance of race and socioeconomic status. In *The Declining Significance of Race*, William Wilson (1978) charged that economic class now is a more salient factor than race in determining life chances for blacks. Charles Vert Willie (1979), in *Caste and Class Controversy*, directly rebutted Wilson. Willie argued that Wilson's work is part of a series of publications (e.g., U.S. Labor Department 1965; Jencks 1972) that obscures the importance of the freedom movement among racial/ethnic minorities. The significance of race is increasing, Willie maintains, especially for middle-class blacks who, because of integration programs (e.g., school desegregation and affirmative action) "are coming into contact with whites for the first time for extended action" (1979: 157). While conceding positive opportunities through desegregation, there are also new opportunities for prejudice and discrimination that have not existed under conditions of segregation.

Social class is important in socialization since early child-rearing practices and resources are fundamental, and these vary with social class (e.g., Kohn 1963). Basic cognitive structures, language styles, and value orientations that children absorb within the family may be expected to vary with ethnicity as well as social class (Bernstein 1964). Johnson and Sanday (1971) found striking differences between blacks and whites at low income levels in value themes. Blacks were lower on "trust in people," "future orienta-tion," and "individual responsibility for poverty."

Between middle-class minorities and middle-class whites, there are not significant differences. For example, in my study of moral judgment in Chicano, black, and white young adults, no significant differences among ethnic categories were found (Cortese 1984b). Subjects were college students, typically from middle-class back-grounds. This suggests that ethnicity is less powerful in the middle class than in the classes below it. Why? In the process of social mo-bility, the formerly lower-class people who are now mobile have tended to move into the 'mainstream' of economic life and thus ac-quired an upper-middle-class lifestyle. This seems to be true of blacks and people of Hispanic origin:

> Black and Spanish [-language] ethnicity do not seem to correlate well with upper-middle-class lifestyle, and therefore they have less influence on the behavior of middle-class blacks and Americans of Spanish origin, though they are relatively stronger than social class influences among the lower-working class (Havighurst 1976: 62).

Upwardly mobile Chicanos, however, do not give up their ethnic identification significantly (Peñalosa and McDonagh 1966). It seems to be the shedding of lower-class culture rather than ethnicity which is most related to upward mobility. Lack of opportunity may delay or preclude development of certain "social skills." This leads us to how differential socialization relates to moral judgment.

Bartz and Levine (1978: 714) found that Chicano parents were similar to blacks in that both expected their children to assume ear-lier responsibility for their behavior more than did Anglos. But al-though Chicano parents expect early autonomy, the father's decision appears to be non-negotiable. This pattern could engender unilateral respect in children. Consequently, the process toward au-tonomous morality is impeded.

To be sure, the Chicano has been influenced by technology and the Anglo culture, yet she or he retains the core values of Mexican folk culture and rejects the basic aspects of the dominant value sys-tem (Hayden 1966: 19). Murillo (1971: 99) states: "Latin values are more closely adhered to than is common in the Anglo culture." Per-haps the availability of recognizable guidelines provides more emo-tional security and a sense of belonging to its members (Ulibarri 1966). A moral judgment scale for Chicanos must respond to a Chicano value orientation that strongly emphasizes interpersonal relations rather than individual rights, abstract principles, law and order, or self-chosen principles.

Various critiques of Kohlberg (e.g., Simpson 1974; Gilligan 1982) suggest that the structures of moral reasoning used by Western middle- to upper-middle-class white males appear to be taken to be everyone's ideal type by many researchers. Similarly, the norms of the dominant culture are taken as the model for the entire society. Moynihan provided a parallel example in his report on the black family. He suggested that the slow rate of progress by blacks resulted from an alleged matriarchal family structure which is "so out of line with the rest of American society" (U.S. Department of Labor 1965: 29). This implied that if black families were made over in the image of white families, they might be treated like whites (Willie 1983). Jensen (1969: 3) provided another example in regard to intelligence: "The remedy deemed logical for children who would do poorly in school is to boost their IQ's up to where they can perform like the majority. . . . " The implication is clear once again; if black children would think like white children, then black children would be treated like white children. But how ethnic and lower-class groups reason morally may be how they should, given their existential condition.

There are at least two ideal types: those of the dominants and those of the subdominants (Willie 1983). Both contribute to the structure and process of social organization, since culture is a composite of ideal types. The norms and contributions of neither may be ignored. For example, the introduction of large numbers of black women into the labor force set a precedent for an increasing number of white women being employed outside the home. In 1900, approximately 4 out of every 10 black women were members of the labor force, a proportion far greater than that for whites (Feagin 1967: 23). The large ratio of black women who work outside the home relative to white women has been often considered as over-representative. But if black women have been overrepresented in the labor force, then white women clearly have been underrepresented (Willie 1983).

I have sketched out several of the ways in which subcultural background (e.g., ethnicity, race, social class) may have a differential effect on individuals during the course of human development. Next I will turn to a critique of cognitive development theory, with special reference to Kohlberg's claim that moral stages are universal. His conceptualization of postconventional morality receives particular scrutiny because of its alleged absence in rural non-Western pre-industrial societies.

Critique of Cognitive Development Theory

The cognitive development approach to intellectual reasoning (Piaget 1952) has been accused of cultural bias (Mangan 1978). Kohlberg's model has also been sharply criticized for the same reason (Simpson 1974; Snarey 1985). The time periods Piaget assigned for the emergence of each stage apparently becomes less applicable the further one is removed from the locale of Piaget's children in Geneva (Bronfenbrenner 1970). Likewise, Kohlberg's theory and method have been accused of favoring white, middle-class Americans, the primary focus of his original theory-building study (Kohlberg 1958).

Cross-national research suggests that the rate and final stage of moral development is highly variable from one cultural setting to another. Individuals in highly industrialized settings are reported to move through the lower stages at a more rapid rate and to achieve higher stages than do individuals in less industrialized and less urban settings. Cultural complexity is salient since greater societal complexity is linked to higher stages of moral development (Edwards 1975).

Simpson (1974), Sullivan (1977), Sullivan et al. (1975), Gilligan (1977, 1982), Gilligan and Murphy (1979), Murphy and Gilligan (1980), and Shweder (1982) have critiqued either Kohlberg's theory or his method as basically impaired or biased. Sullivan (1977) views Kohlberg's theory as a liberal ideology rooted in certain sociohistorical conditions. This includes an idea that humans are essentially rational, a focus on justice and individual rights, and a commitment to the concept of social contract. Yet his highest Stage 6 reasoning is in fact parochial, not universal, Sullivan claims. Kohlberg assumes a fair and just society; he does not consider injustice in contemporary society. Sullivan draws from Marx, Engels, and Lukacs to criticize Kohlberg's "abstract formalism." The focus on form comes from the form–content distinction central to structural stage psychology (Kohlberg 1984). When formalism is applied to ethics correctness of choice is determined from the universal form of the principle followed. According to formalism, the adequacy of an ethnical stance can be agreed upon according to its structure without having to reach consensus on the substance of its ethical values.

In one sense, formalism can be viewed as conservative ideology because it supports the *status quo* and an unconscious "defense of exploitation" (Sullivan 1977). In separating form and content, cognition and behavior, Kohlberg erroneously equates the more complex and abstract with the more right and moral. There is a lack of emotion, moral sensitivity, and imagination in Kohlberg's theory. The theory is incomplete and reflects an ideological bias rooted in Western culture. The use of false dichotomies results in an alienated and "morally blind" perspective on persons as moral agents.

Simpson (1974), like Sullivan, disputes Kohlberg's stages as culturally universal. There is a dearth of postconventional (Stages 5 and 6) scores in underdeveloped and rural cultures. If postconventional reasoning is more prevalent in urban cultures that are Western-influenced, then it follows that Kohlberg's invariant stage sequence, particularly the conceptualizing and operationalizing of the highest stages, is culturally biased and ethnocentric. On philosophical and empirical grounds, one can criticize the claim of cultural universality. Empirically, there is a lack of postconventional reasoning in the protocols of individuals in virtually all Third World cultures. Moreover, regression to "lower" stages has been found in some individuals in various cultures, even Americans (Colby et al. 1983).

Furthermore, the measures are methodologically problematical. The scarcity or absence of postconventional reasoning in some cultures may not mirror actual disparity in moral judgment. Instead, it can reflect differences that occur due to a lack of understanding the background of subjects. Thus the researcher needs to be more sensitive to the conditions that affect performance during the Moral Judgment Interview. Recalling three examples illustrates this. First, a "postconventional" score could represent the subject's linguistic sophistication, not the individual's underlying stage structure. The concepts expressed by subjects at Stage 5 depend on a high level of abstraction that would automatically exclude most people, including many American adults. Next, the moral dilemmas are presented in a constraining interview situation; they may not be a familiar or relevant context in which to gauge moral thinking. Finally, the interviewer, translator, scorer, or researcher's insensitivity to cultural meanings could result in the misinterpretation or devaluation of responses from other cultures. To avoid misinterpreting the reasoning of culturally diverse subjects, the scoring manual needs to include indigenous examples of reasoning at higher stages (Kohlberg, Snarey, and Reimer 1984).

A research-based scale of development cannot be applied objectively or universally; it is a product of a certain cultural background at a particular point in time. The genesis of Kohlberg's instrument in modern Western society and ideology, despite the claim of universality, allows invidious comparisons between cultures; the stage sequence implies a scale for grading some cultures as "morally superior," others as "morally deficient." Development theorists use infant mortality rates, education, income equality, gender equality, and caloric intake as non-psychological tests of societal development. It is my position that societies may be high in political complexity, but also high in infant mortality and ethnic, educational, income, and gender inequality. Consequently, a high degree of societal complexity does not necessarily mean a high degree of societal morality.

Schweder (1982) also criticizes the claim of universality. Morality is historically and culturally relativistic. Moral standards may be like language and food, different across cultures but still equal in usefulness and applicability. Attempts since the Enlightment to develop a rational basis for a objective universal ethic have in fact been constructed out of non-rational presuppositions, premises which any rational person could reasonably deny (MacIntyre 1982). Rational foundations turn out to be the soft sand of preferred, and often widely shared, assumptions. At its limits, moral discourse becomes ideology, a deceptive "mock rationality."

Kohlberg is ultimately unable to separate content and form. Further, contrary to Kohlberg's theory, there is no formal similarity of moral reasoning at the postconventional stages. Kohlberg's conceptualization of justice is a form of liberal ideology, faithfully endorsed by secular humanists but not required by reason or fact. The data appear to bear out Kohlberg's assumption that Third World societies are inferior. There is a dearth of Stage 5 and 6 reasoning in non-Western and especially rural societies. Nevertheless, the assumptions' partiality toward astract moral principles and societal complexity undermines the theory. Finally, the data do not support the Piagetian assumptions of invariant stage sequence and structural wholeness. Moral reasoning seems to be more multidimensional than Kohlberg has implied (Cortese 1987).

Kohlberg's attempt to construct a rational basis for an objectively valid morality is founded on non-rational premises (e.g., a belief in "equal and universal rights," the view that they are "natural" rights, a focus on "humanity" in general rather than to one's tribe, community, or nation, a rejection of the exercise of power, influ-

ence, and force, and a relinquishing of emphasis on differences between people—ethnicity, age, sex, intelligence, lineage—when
determining how to treat them). Such notions are substantive, not
abstract. An objective, rational morality based on logically comprehensive principles of justice (e.g., human rights) is not possible because the notion of "human rights" has not been operationalized
nor agreed upon. There is no universal scale for balancing human
rights. There are no exchange counters to which to bring one's personal principles and trade them for equivalent universal principles.
There are no objective standards by which to weigh the actions of
ourselves and others.

Feminist Critique of Cognitive Development Theory

Carol Gilligan (1982) provides a "sweeping critique of all major developmental theories on the grounds that they are biased against
women" (Colby and Damon 1983: 474). She attacks Freud, Piaget,
and Kohlberg for defining morality as "justice." Longitudinal analysis of Kohlberg's original sample (e.g., Colby et al. 1983) has provided the data for theoretical revision, but longitudinal data
analysis of females did not occur until 1969.

Kohlberg (1984) acknowledged the importance of an orientation
of care, connectedness, and responsibility in moral reasoning. He
also admits that the scoring manual (Colby et al. 1987) does not lead
to a complete assessment of this orientation. Gilligan suggests that
this type of moral reasoning is used predominantly by females,
while males tend to use a rights or justice orientation. Theoretically,
if women do not participate in society's secondary institutions
(through education and work responsibility), they are not likely to
acquire those role-taking abilities necessary for the progression to
the higher stages. Kohlberg's framework (especially the postconventional level) "reflects a limited Western male perspective and may
therefore be biased against women and other groups whose moral
perspectives are somewhat different" (Gilligan 1982: 36). Using
Kohlberg's standard dilemmas, individuals' regression in prescriptive reasoning about justice in early adulthood was found (Gilligan
and Murphy 1979; Murphy and Gilligan 1980). Conversely, there
was also developmental progression on real-life dilemmas. The responsibility dimension is more context-relevant than the justice orientation, and relies on relative contextual perceptions of the factual
moral situation and its psychological consequences. Postconventional morality is viewed as an adolescent type of overly theoretical

and overly abstract moral perception that potentially is transformed into a contextually relative morality in adulthood.

While the work of Gilligan (1982) is consistent with the assumptions of cognitive development theory, there is strong criticism of the "long established pattern in academic research of establishing norms based on men's experience alone" (Kerber et al. 1986: 305). (Note that Kohlberg's original six-stage theory of moral judgment emerged from an all-male sample.) It is the content of the stages— particularly Stages 3 and 4—that is considered to be gender-biased. The traits that commonly have identified female virtues, their care for and sensitivity to the needs of others, are those that by Kohlberg's moral criteria label women as deficient in moral development. Recall that Gilligan uses the psychoanalytical framework of Nancy Chodorow (1978), which points to gender differences very early in life. Girls initially develop connection with their mothers, while boys initially develop separation from their mothers. It follows that:

Adolescent boys need to learn to manage relationships despite their basic and central sense of separation and individuality while girls must struggle to establish a separate identity while maintaining relationships (Kerber et al. 1986: 305).

These assumptions, however, are problematic. First, it is not clear that girls develop a sense of connection before boys. According to the cognitive development assumption of hierarchical integration, males must incorporate Stage 3 connectedness before "progressing" to the rules orientation of Stage 4. Conversely, it is also not evident that boys develop a sense of separation and individuality before girls. A separate identity is necessary in order to function even at the preconventional level (Stages 1 and 2).

Gilligan has been criticized for basing her conclusions on "a study of women—and only women—confronting a decision about abortion" (Kerber et al. 1986: 305). Is she not just as guilty as Kohlberg is for using an all-male sample? No. The preponderance of the care orientation in the protocols of women is enough to demonstrate the incompleteness of Kohlberg's approach. Research on moral judgment reasoning as "justice" has been well documented.

This is where Gilligan's critics who question the existence of gender differences in moral judgment (Walker 1984; Kerber et al. 1986) miss the point. The point is that Gilligan has expanded the domain of moral judgment by showing that woman define themselves through their relationships with others, focusing on care and intimacy rather than separation and achievement. If we define morality according to conceptions of justice and systems of rules that are more attainable by one segment of the population than others—whether that segment is based on gender, race, ethnicity, or social class—this notion of morality is probably biased. Consequently, the presumed retardation and deficiencies in female development result from problems inherent in Kohlberg's theory and research methodology.

Whether there are gender differences in moral reasoning is not the major issue. More important is the point that different people perceive moral dilemmas differently and that these differences may be linked not only to intrapsychic tendencies, but also to real life experiences. For example, women tend to be made more anxious than men by the isolation involved in achievement, while men tend to be more anxious by intimacy (Pollak and Gilligan 1982).

While the debate continues over gender differences in moral reasoning, let us assume, for the sake of argument, that Gilligan's critics are correct—that there are no such significant differences in moral judgment when controlled for social class and education. (My own research has found a great deal of overlap between female and male responses to the Kohlberg dilemmas in terms of the care and justice orientations.) Kohlberg's measures are too narrow to conclude that there are no gender differences. Given the all-male sample on which Kohlberg's theory is based and the inability of the research methodology to effectively tap the care orientation, one must look beyond one specific type of research program to satisfactorily answer this major question. If women are different from men in moral judgment, are black women different from white women? Are middle-class women different from lower- or upper-class women? Are black woman similar to black men?

Under conditions of economic deprivation there is a convergence based on similarity in class positions between women and men in their self-definition, in their definition of relationships with others, and in their definition of morality, justice, responsibility, and social good. The contextualizing of morality and of the meaning of social relationships and responsibilities found in my ethnic/racial minority subjects represents a cultural explanation that is an alternative to both Gilligan's and Kohlberg's models of moral development. My objective is to make readers conscious of the importance of ethnicity, race, and class, as well as gender, in the social construction of morality. Consequently, multicultural approaches to morality broaden the narrow focus of research on justice reasoning and open up avenues to studying different interpretations of reciprocity, of commitment to family, friendship, community, national and international ties, and of care and responsibility components of morality. Gilligan acknowledges that the focus on care in moral reasoning is not characteristic of all woman. Rather it seems to be limited to females in advantaged populations. Consequently, ethnicity, race, and social class are more basic than gender in shaping one's conceptions of self and morality.

Indeed, gender is established by the existential experience of ethnicity, race, culture, social class, caste and consciousness. Gilligan (Kerber et al. 1986: 326) has effectively argued that "what had been missed by leaving out women [in moral judgment research] was a different way of constituting the idea of the self and the idea of what is moral." It is important to note that Gilligan's "different voice" is identified not by gender but by theme. Gilligan depended on a close textual analysis of language and logic in claiming that common themes recur in women's conceptions of self and morality. Woman are less likely than men to reason at the postconventional level of morality because they are less likely to define moral dilemmas in terms of abstract, universal principles of justice. The point is that low scores on standard moral judgment indices do not necessarily mean less ethical development; instead, it may signal a qualitatively distinct approach to moral problem solving based on ethnic background, culture, or gender. Gilligan (1982) provides an empirical example of how inadequate Kohlberg's framework, with its stress on "justice reasoning," is for both a male and a female adolescent. What might seem to be a basic conflict of rights, and therefore a simple exercise in moral logic, becomes a much more complex and multidimensional situation.

Besides gender differences in moral orientations, Pollak and Gilligan (1982) have reported differences in the incidence and interpretation of violent fantasies in women and men. A greater percentage of the men in their sample related violence to close, personal affiliation, perceiving danger in intimacy. A smaller percentage of woman wrote stories containing violent acts; most linked violence with competitive success, and construed violence as resulting from separation and isolation from relationships (Pollak and Gilligan 1982: 161). Pollak and Gilligan's conclusions have been criticized as "potentially damaging information that might be uncritically presented to and adopted by the public as fact" (Benton et al. 1983:

1171), by providing data which "justify" the continuation of "repressive stereotypes regarding men and women" (Benton et al. 1983: 1167). But careful study of the content of the stories written by subjects points to a generally positive and active picture of women: "The inclusion of women's experience dispels the view of care as selfless and passive and reveals the activities that constitute care and lead to responsiveness in human relationships" (Kerber et al. 1986: 332).

At this point let us review some of the basic points in the feminist critique of cognitive development theory. The previous chapter noted that Gilligan (1982) raises the issue that some people, particularly women, do not define morality in terms of justice, universality, fairness, or logical comprehensiveness unlike Kant, Rawls, and Kohlberg. Instead, she proposes, moral reasoning includes a dimension often overlooked by Kohlberg. Some people focus on responsibility, concern for others, and practicality, supporting the assumption that moral judgments do not occur in a temporal or social void. Rather, moral inferences and choices are made in the context of everyday circumstances that confront an individual. While the principle orientation of Stage 6 reasoning is objective, responsibility perspectives are often action-oriented and intersubjective. That is, Kohlberg's highest and most adequate stage centers on a logical comprehensiveness that promotes autonomy and sets up moral problems as a mathematical equation. Conversely, such logic is not relevant to the individual in real-life dilemmas. Instead, moral solutions emphasize the interdependence of people's lives. In short, the type of moral judgment central to cognitive development theory is but one of several possible modes of analysis. The basic question is not whether women are different from men but rather how are care, responsibility, and interpersonal orientations to morality synthesized with rules and rights orientations.

There are also recent developments in critical social theory (Benhabib 1986) that oppose the normative foundation of Kohlberg's theory. Seyla Benhabib approaches Kohlberg indirectly, through Habermas. She uses Hegel's critique of Kant to question the attempt by Habermas to base the epistemological underpinnings of critical theory upon a "communicative ethics." For Hegel, the objective is to advance the synthesis of the morally autonomous person into an ethical community. In this view, the contribution by Habermas to a critique of society is the refocusing of critical theory, from "the [Hegelian] model of a subject of work" (Benhabib 1986: xi), to communicative action. Habermas regards autonomy as communicative competence in structuring and justifying moral judgment and conduct on a universalistic basis. The cognitive developmental assumption that moral stages are culturally universal is what attracts Habermas to Kohlberg and upon which he rests his model. Habermas's communicative model assumes that social action should be construed in terms of the subject-subject (vis-à-vis subject–object) relationship.

Habermas uses Kohlberg to characterize the ideal speech situation. Habermas's "communicative ethics" is very similar to Kohlberg's Stage 6. The applicability of universal ethical principles has been questioned because it ignores the context of real-life moral problems. Even Habermas and Kohlberg acknowledge that the hypothetical moral capacity examined by the cognitive development frameworks is not close to the corresponding moral capacity in actual situations. They nevertheless maintain that there must be logical justification of moral principles in addition to their applicability in particular contexts. Consequently, they claim that it is correct to make a distinction between justification and contexutalization. The integration of the critical theory of Habermas and the cognitive developmental theory of Kohlberg is the focus of Chapter 7.

The Ethnic Context of Moral Stages

The question of whether ethnic background affects moral development in American children and young adults has not been of major concern to researchers. Yet the value of Kohlberg's (1969) approach, beyond its theoretical argument, is its claim of the consistent performance by individuals across diverse linguistic and cultural settings. But Kohlberg's stages are insensitive to particular ethnic backgrounds. Comparative ethnic studies are crucial in assessing the validity and reliability of the cognitive development model and its corresponding research instruments.

Does ethnicity have an effect of its own, independent of the effects of other background variables? Do ethnic groups progress in moral development at the same rate by age or grade level? Results of my moral judgment studies of Chicano, black, and white children (Cortese, 1980, 1982a, 1982b) suggest that these groups generally do not progress at the same rate by age. Whites scored highest in all five areas of moral reasoning studied.

Ethnic background appears to have its greatest effect on level of moral judgment in the following two dimensions. First of all, ethnicity is the key factor in level of moral realism. Higher scores are especially associated with older middle-class whites. In level of communicable responsibility, ethnic background as a main effect is significant. Accordingly, "higher" responses are related to middle-class whites, non-Catholics, and older students. Chicanos and blacks make up the largest proportion of preconventional responses; whites have the greatest ratio of conventional answers. Moreover, 83% of the few postconventional scores were given by whites. Analysis of ethnic background by grade level for each of the five moral judgment variables shows that these ethnic groups generally do not progress in moral development at the same rate by age. By every measure, whites are inclined to score "higher" than Chicanos or blacks.

Considering possible ethnic differences in moral judgment, any of the following explanations might be offered (Edwards 1981): Cultural differences result from a bias built into the definition of the stages; cultural differences result from variations in social experience that stimulate moral growth by encouraging processes of role taking; apparent cultural differences result from a misguided attempt to capture multidimensional cultural variation on a unidimensional scale; cultural differences result from poor testing procedures.

Stage Bias

Cultural differences in moral judgment would vanish if the stage definitions were reconstructed to be more culturally content-free. The present stages focus on a core value of fairness defined as reciprocity, equality, and individuality. These central concepts may be appropriate for respondents with a Western European background but not for Chicanos or blacks. Different moral judgment scales, all based on social role taking, could be developed around different core values. The major concern for moral judgment research on ethnic minorities is how rapidly the children proceed toward a more complex goal or final stage of morality rather than their progress in "universal" moral development.

Social Experience and Role Taking

According to cognitive development theory, low scores on moral judgment measures by ethnic minority children indicate that such children generally have not been exposed to the types of moral problems that encourage them to take on the role of the generalized other as they seek appropriate solutions to such problems and concurrently progress through the stages of development. Socialization and role-taking experience affect cognitive development through family and peer group activity, shared exposure to the media, common reading experience, formal associations, in-group marriage, and residential segregation. For the ethnic minority child, the ability to survive in a particular environment has taught subcultural beliefs and value complexes that are not likely to be counteracted in the developmental process (e.g., the barrio child at Stage 2 whose existential beliefs are grounded in a reality of instrumental relativism). Lack of opportunity may delay or preclude the development of various other types of social "skills." This deficiency in the less "complex" cultures is not due to biological inferiority, but rather to a lack of specific role-taking experiences resulting from social dilemmas that stimulate reasoning at the "higher" stages of moral development.

Multidimensionality of Moral Judgment

Cultural differences in stage sequences represent a distortion and oversimplification of reality. They have no proper place in the examination of cultural variation in normative thought (Simpson 1974). Fundamental social and cultural influences are likely to be at work where a slower rate of progression in moral development for ethnic minority children is evident. Success in registering "higher" levels of moral judgment depends on familiarity with methods of analyzing the physical and social realms that are not pan-cultural.

Methodological Criteria

The previous chapter proposed that moral dilemmas must involve values pertinent to the culture of the subjects. For Chicanos, as an example, this means (1) either adapting the original dilemmas or creating new ones appropriate for Chicanos. Research procedures must be designed to elicit the best, most reflective reasoning of Chicanos; (2) in interviews, oral rather than written responses are generally most pertinent; (3) dilemmas and probing questions must be presented in the first language of the subject—if the interview is administered in Spanish, answers should be written and scored in Spanish or else translated with as little distortion as possible into English for scoring. These three criteria require bilingual proficiency and thorough knowledge of Chicano culture.

My moral judgment research on Chicano, black, and white young middle-class adults (Cortese 1984b, 1987) revealed few differences between ethnic groups in regard to stage structure. Seventy-eight percent of all subjects (or 65 percent to 80 percent within each ethnic category) scored at Stage 3 or Stage 3/4. Combining the highest two (4 and 4/5) or three (3/4, 4, and 4/5) stages, whites scored higher than Chicanos and blacks. Using those same categories, males scored higher than females. The average stage for whites and for males was 3/4. Black and Chicano women were typically at Stage 3. Within each category, a pattern of gender differences becomes more clear; males scored at least one-half stage higher than females for all three racial/ethnic categories. The results of a multiple regression analysis indicate that age appears to have the greatest impact on global stage score, followed by the effects of ethnicity and social class. The finding that age was positively associated with the level of moral judgment supports Piaget's ([1932] 1965) theoretical proposition.

Differences between ethnic groups can be at least partially explained as due to a theoretical bias favoring white middle-class values. The ethnic differences led me to seek possible empirical support for disparities in the socialization process of ethnic groups which may in turn affect moral development. I take the position that moral development is multi-dimensional and is the most salient factor in ethnic differences. Consequently, moral judgment models and indicators must take into account the personal, social, and cultural context of moral development when assessing an individual's moral maturity. Such dimensions include, but are not necessarily limited to, moral conduct, the affective component of moral reasoning, situational and subcultural factors, and judgments made to justify or excuse previous behavior.

Although there were ethnic differences in moral judgment between children, there was not much disparity in stages of moral development between ethnic categories in the adult sample. Perhaps ethnic background has a more profound effect upon individuals during the childhood years when family activity, language spoken in the home, linguistic concepts, in-group socialization, and social segregation are more likely to shape the belief systems and behavior of members. As the child matures, self-identity transcends ethnic boundaries. Peer group constraints and pressures become especially strong. Educational, occupational, and social status aspirations derived from media influences may replace a social identity that has a significant ethnic component. Ethnic minority young adults begin to become more middle-class, at least cognitively, if not behaviorally. These results are consistent with those where comparisons of ethnic minorities with whites at middle-class levels have not revealed significant differences. In the process of acculturation, ethnic minority individuals give up, to varying degrees, their native culture and acquire the dominant American culture. It is typically the culture of the more powerful group that will be learned. Acculturation, however, does not necessarily lead to acceptance of the ethnic minority by the dominant group.

Moral judgment has an implicit political bias: it is confined by the structure of social relations. Moral development is structural, not psychological. Kohlberg states that moral development rests on abstract, logically comprehensive, and culturally universal principles of justice. But people are more important than principles. Future research should focus on the diversity of social transmission, a key factor in Piaget's original theory. Specifically, variables such as a cooperative or competitive orientation, parental support and/or control, and types of family authority would seem to offer promise.

While the works of Piaget and Kohlberg are of monumental importance for the study of moral judgment and moral behavior, there is a major flaw in their works. The assertion that there are six and only six stages with one and only one final, mature mode of moral judgment preempts all other moral systems for all time. An alternative view is that each ethnic group constructs a sequence for moral development and a mode of moral judgment appropriate to its own culture which are morally neither superior nor inferior to the cognitive development model. Rather, in that diverse social ends are sought, they simply are different.

One must consider the possibility that ethnic groups have different moral structures, each adequate to the reproduction of the social life-world found in each ethnic group. One must also consider the possibility that the "scientific findings" on moral development are more appropriately viewed as ideology that sets the Western European social life-world as the model for all people in all places. Finally, one must consider the possibility that morality is located more in the structure of society than it is in the consciousness of individual human beings. If this possibility is valid, then measures of moral development need to focus on quality of life variables found in a given society or social class or subculture within a society, rather than upon individuals' oral or written replies to hypothetical dilemmas. There is much to do in the course of building adequate theory on and measuring moral development. The first task is to sort out all the political bias built into existing research.

Cross-Cultural Research: The Link to Ethnic Moral Styles

Thus far, the argument presented here has been concerned with examining ethnic differences in moral judgment within the United States. But let us expand this investigation to the cross-cultural evidence presented to support Kohlberg's theory. It will suggest that the problems associated with moral judgment studies of ethnic and racial groups in the United States are quite similar to those for other cultures, again using excerpts from my moral judgment interviews. The evidence does not strongly support the universal validity of Kohlberg's moral stages.

There have been 45 studies in 26 cultural areas conducted to test the cultural universality of Kohlberg's moral stages. A recent review of these studies has identified some major caveats regarding the range and general applicability of the stages across cultures (Snarey 1985). Specifically, biases in favor of complex urban societies and middle-class populations were identified. The cultural universality of moral development rests on five assumptions: (1) culturally diverse samples; (2) universal moral questions; (3) invariant sequence of stages; (4) a full range of stages; and (5) general applicability.

Social and Cultural Diversity

Moral development research should represent a wide range of sociocultural settings. Moreover, within these settings, there should be internally diverse samples (i.e., children, adolescents, and adults; males and females; subjects at all levels of social stratification). Since Standard Form Scoring (Colby et al. 1987) is the only method with established validity and reliability, earlier studies using previous methods cannot be used to evaluate the theory's worth. Even so, there are also validity and reliability problems with Standard Form Scoring (Cortese 1984a), as noted in Chapter 4. Similarly, since interrater reliability is crucial to the scoring system, those studies that do not test for and report it also cannot be used to assess its validity.

There are only six cultural settings besides the United States (Colby et al. 1983) where Standard Form Scoring was used and interrater reliability reported: The Bahamas (White, Bushnell, and Regnemer 1978); Israel (Snarey, Reimer, and Kohlberg 1985); Taiwan (Lei and Chung 1984); Turkey (Nisan and Kohlberg 1982; Turiel, Edwards, and Kohlberg 1978); New Guinea (Tietjen and Walker 1984); and Kenya (Harkness, Edwards, and Super 1981). Only males were interviewed in two of these sociocultural settings, Turkey and New Guinea, violating the requirement of internally diverse samples (e.g., male and female subjects). In addition, in the Kenyan study, the lowest interrater reliability (.77), the smallest sample size (n = 12), and no postconventional scores (Stages 4/5 and 5) are reported. This was only a case study: scores did not cover the full range of moral stages. Consequently, evidence for the cultural universality of moral stages rests, incredibly, on only three non-U.S. settings, the Bahamas, Israel, and Taiwan. There is a strong need for more studies using culturally and ethnically diverse subjects, Standard Form Scoring, and interrater reliability to assess the cultural universality of moral stages.

Universal Moral Questions and Invariant Stage Sequence

Moral judgment studies should demonstrate that all persons are asked the same kinds of questions and can resort to the same basic issues in solving dilemmas. (This was discussed in Chapter 4 as a component on ecological validity.) Moral stages should form an invariant sequence. (Evidence on this was discussed in Chapter 4.)

Range of Stages

The full range of moral stages should be found in all types of cultures. Stages 4/5 and 5 were absent in every traditional tribal or village folk society whether Western or non-Western. There are significant differences in moral judgment between folk and urban societies, not between Western and non-Western ones (Redfield 1956, 1962; Edwards 1975). In addition, Snarey's (1985) review of socially stratified samples from ten of eleven countries showed significant class differences in moral development. In each case, upper-middle- or middle-class subjects scored higher than lower-class or working-class subjects. In the United States, class differences were common, and virtually always favored the middle class in terms of higher stages of moral judgment (DeVos 1983).

All of the non-Western samples with postconventional subjects (India, Israeli, kibbutz, Taiwan) were from modern societies, including two with urban communities. All of the non-Western samples that failed to score beyond the conventional level (Kenyan village leaders, Tibetan monks, New Guinea village leaders) were from traditional folk societies. Differences in moral judgment by social class and societal type suggest a bias in the scoring system.

General Applicability

All examples of moral reasoning in all cultures should correspond to one of the moral stages; there is no wastebasket or "other" category. But protocols of subjects from the Israeli kibbutz (Snarey 1982), India (Vasudev 1983), Taiwan (Lei and Chung 1984), Papua New Guinea (Tietjen and Walker 1984), and Kenya (Edwards 1986) reveal principles and moral reasoning not included in Kohlberg's six moral stages. These include postconventional principles of communal equality and collective happiness (kibbutz); cooperation, nonviolence, and the unity of all life, human and non-human (India); filial piety, collective utility (Taiwan and New Guinea); and unity, respect, and understanding (Kenya). Guess scores were sometimes used, indicating genuine moral judgments not found in the scoring manual. Some judgments of kibbutz subjects which were scored as guess Stage 4 or guess Stage 4/5 could have been pure Stage 5 judgments if the rater took a socialist kibbutz perspective rather than a middle-class capitalistic perspective (Snarey 1985).

The principle of the unity of all life, expressed by some of my ethnic minority subjects (Cortese 1984b) and by an Indian subject (Vasudev 1983), was only evident when a question regarding the value of non-human life was asked (i.e., Should Heinz steal the drug to save his pet animal?). This may point to a difference in the ethical frameworks of non-Western European and Western European backgrounds. The following responses to that question by some of my ethnic minority and women subjects lend credence to the notion that moral situations are not limited to relations between humans:

> No. 13 (black male): That's an interesting question. From my point of view, yes. The animal has just as much right to be on the face of this earth as human beings do; we're animals also.
> No. 11 (white female): Yes. Especially if it's a dog. I love animals and I believe they should be treated the same as humans.
> No. 15 (black male): Yes. It's something he loves. He doesn't love everything, but he loves his pet. He wants to keep it instead of getting a new one.
> No. 25 (Chicano female): Yes. It's still a living creature.
> No. 2 (black male): It might not be ethical to some people, but a pet might be a very dear thing to you.
> No. 23 (black female): It's another life, a living organism, and he loves it that much.

In contrast, a white male who supported Heinz's stealing the drug even if he doesn't love his wife or for a stranger since "All life is sacred" and "All life in and of itself is worth maintaining," did not favor stealing for a pet:

> Question: If Heinz doesn't love his wife, should he steal the drug for her?
> No. 1 Yes. All life is sacred. Your like or dislike has nothing to do with it. Life in and of itself is worth maintaining.

Q.: Should Heinz steal the drug for the stranger?
An.: Yes. All life is worth maintaining.
Q.: Should Heinz steal to save a pet animal?
A.: Okay, I qualify the things I mentioned before in terms of human life. Human life, I believe, has a higher value than animal life. So I would say, "No." He should not steal the drug for an animal's life.

None of the white males and only one of the white females favored stealing the drug to save a pet:

No. 41 (white male): It's an animal; he can just get another one, whereas a human life—you can't. Not as easy, at least.

No. 37 (white male): Just because animals aren't as important as people.

No. 3 (white male): I think only human life would be worth stealing for.

No. 50 (white female): Human life and animal life are on two different levels.

No. 24 (white male): You can be attached to animals but they're not as valuable as a person is.

Subjects sometimes reply to the open-ended moral questions in a narrative style, by telling a parable or a story. This is especially common in India since narration is a major mode of moral discourse in Hindu society. In narrative style, subjects respond to a question with, "Let me tell you a story," and proceed to tell a moral tale from which the interviewer is expected to draw a lesson. Even highly trained scorers were unable to score this type of interview material (Snarey 1985). The storyteller shifts from respondent (explaining personal reasoning) to teacher (trying to stimulate the interviewer's reasoning).

Two black subjects in my sample (Cortese 1984b) used the narrative style to answer questions:

Question: Thinking in terms of society, should people who break the law be punished?

No. 13: It depends on the situation. Some people who break the law should be punished. Some people have moral reasons for breaking the law. I can cite a case down in Denver where a black male who had been laid off (and has a family of five and a wife) robbed a King Soopers store. He got all the groceries that he could for his children and turned himself in the next day. He went to the judge and told him exactly why he did it, and told him, "Hey, I'll serve time, but I was not going to stand there and let my family starve." The judge suspended his sentence.

Q.: The father promised Joe he could go to camp if he earned the money. Is the fact that the father promised the most important thing in the situation?

A.: Yeah.

Q.: Why?

A.: I've never been a parent, but I'm from a family of six (with my parents). We were raised in the same pattern as in this story. I had to save up my money to get my first bike. My parents didn't make that much money. We were dependent but we had to understand that there was also independence. If you wanted something badly, you had to go out and get it. And if you got it —then fine, your parents congratulated you and worked with you. The love was not lost, but there was a lot more self-determination gained.

Question: Is it important to keep a promise?

No. 30 (black female): I think so.

Q.: Why?

A.: It's like the story about the little boy who cried wolf and kept crying wolf. The last time he cried wolf, nobody came to his rescue. That's like a promise. If you promise to pay back some money to someone and you don't pay them back, chances are you won't be able to borrow from that person.

Filial piety, as expressed by Taiwanese subjects, is represented in Criterion Judgments given at Stage 3 (affiliation norm), not Stage 5. Indeed, most collectivist moral principles, the link between human relationships and society, are completely omitted in the scoring manual. Some village leaders in New Guinea placed blame for the Heinz dilemma on the community: "If nobody helped him [to save his dying wife] and so he [stole to save her], I would say we had caused that problem" (Tietjen and Walker 1984: 21). Stage 4 should require only "a rough appreciation of society's needs for institutionalized roles, [not] a full-blown understanding of organizational aspects of a social structure and the operation of a legal system" (Edwards 1986: 11).

In conclusion, culturally unique moral judgments from an Israeli kibbutz, India, Taiwan, New Guinea, and Kenya are omitted from the theory and scoring manual. Collective solidarity or communalistic principles, in particular, are missing or misunderstood. Virtually all urban and middle-class samples exhibited principled reasoning, no folk cultural or working-class groups did. Kohlberg's socially evolutionist position is culturally ethnocentric: Individuals in some societies should not be expected to develop Stage 5 reasoning, since they do not possess or experience the cognitive and social prerequisites for such reasoning. Kohlberg's argument is invalid on three grounds (Snarey 1985). First, preliterate people in "primitive " societies do use formal structures to make sense of their world (Lévi-Strauss 1962, 1963). But their thinking is so different from Western cognitive styles that Western linguists and social scientists are sometimes unable to comprehend it in its complexity. Second, role-taking and other social prerequisites of postconventional moral reasoning are indeed experienced by members of tribal or village folk societies. When they experience conflict, for example, between neighboring villages or tribal groups, community leaders must resolve disputes for both groups (Kohlberg's moral reversibility). Third, even in moral judgment scores by Kohlberg's criteria, North American subjects are not, on the average, superior to those of other subjects. Kohlberg's U.S. sample did not rank first in mean moral maturity scores in any age cohort. Taiwanese, kibbutzniks, Indians, and Turkish subjects scored higher than their American counterparts at one or more points in the life cycle.

Conclusion

Different ethnic and sociocultural settings (e.g., the United States) and social systems (e.g., prisons) can be expected to differ in their orientation to moral judgment. Even, if some members of a society express postconventional reasoning, some social systems may prevent or limit its acceptance or operationalizing. In prisons, for instance, it may be dangerous to reason beyond Stage 2. Similarly, the social structure of the United States made it dangerous for Martin Luther King, Jr., to reason beyond Stage 4 (Kohlberg 1981b). Cultural and subcultural world views, by contrast, can be used in moral reasoning at any stage level. There are, for example, varying levels of sophistication within any particular religious tradition despite major differences between it and other religions. "Although every society may not have a significant proportion of its population reasoning at the higher stages, every culture is capable of supporting higher stage reasoning" (Snarey 1985: 228).

The stage definitions and scoring system are incomplete, especially at Stage 5. They should be expanded to include postconventional reasoning from culturally and subculturally diverse world views. This elaboration could reveal Stage 5 to be a more common empirical phenomenon. In short, a more culturally pluralistic stage theory of moral reasoning is needed.

6

Beyond Legitimation: The Judgment of Morality or The Morality of Judgment

> Injustice anywhere is a threat to justice everywhere.
> —*Martin Luther King, Jr.*

> First they came for the Jews
> and I did not speak out—
> because I was not a Jew.
> Then they came for the communists
> and I did not speak out—
> because I was not a communist.
> Then they came for the trade unionists
> and I did not speak out—
> because I was not a trade unionist.
> Then they came for me—
> and there was no one left
> to speak out for me.
> —*Pastor Martin Niemöeller (victim of the Nazis)*

In this chapter, I will expand on the socio-political ramifications of my research findings. I argue that moral development is a tool of mental class domination. Accordingly, I will make a connection between moral development (as conditioned by socioeconomic and racial ethnic background) and ideology. But first I will briefly summarize some of the more important points about the Harvard School of Moral Education. After that, I propose a sociology of moral judgment. I maintain that the end-point of Kohlberg's model is more ideology than science and that morality is more a social phenomenon than a psychological one. Excerpts from the interviews with my research subjects support my thesis and illustrate some of the problems and omissions in Kohlberg's approach. Let us review the moral development school.

The Harvard School of Moral Education

The cognitive development study of moral judgment began in Geneva with Piaget's ([1932] 1965) investigation of children's game rules. Kohlberg (1958) relied on Piaget's theory in a study to identify modes of moral judgment observed in Chicago school children. Further studies followed. Turiel (1966) tested for the sequences of moral stages in children. Kohlberg and Turiel conducted cross-cultural studies to validate the moral stages (Kohlberg 1966, 1969; Turiel 1969; Turiel, Edwards, and Kohlberg 1978). Kohlberg came to Harvard University from the University of Chicago in 1967 (Lawrence Kohlberg, personal correspondence, June 28, 1983).

Under Kohlberg's charismatic leadership and intellectual guidance, a school of moral development was founded at Harvard in the late 1960s (Cortese 1986b). The school was in the vanguard of research on moral cognition. Rest's (1969) dissertation provided support for the hierarchical integration of stage structure. Kohlberg (1969) used data from the experiments by Rest and Turiel and from cross-cultural studies to bolster his theoretical formulations on moral reasoning. This claim countered the behaviorist paradigm that had gained control of psychology in the 1950s and 1960s.

Besides research, the Harvard school became a leading advocate of moral education programs based on the core ideas of the theory. The declaration on developmental research (Kohlberg 1969) preceded an equally programmatic statement using the research findings as a lead into educational policy (Kohlberg 1971b). It was this objective that had brought Kohlberg, Rest, and Blatt from Chicago, and Turiel from Columbia, to Harvard for what eventually became the Center for Moral Education. Kohlberg's approach to morality and socialization provided a new view of social reality. His research has had a major impact on contemporary psychology and education. Kohlberg has also influenced the interpretation of social issues of justice and the implementation of moral education programs.

Despite the strong impact of Kohlberg's proclamation, problems remained. Up to this point, although the theoretical formulations were influential, there was little evidence for moral stages as cognitive development structures. Kohlberg and Kramer (1969), in an analysis of longitudinal data, discovered an excessive number of anomalous cases of regression and stage skipping. After redefining several stages, Kohlberg (1973) was convinced that although there were serious methodological problems, the theory was basically sound. The Harvard School entered a new phase of research. The objective was to establish a valid and reliable method of assessing moral stages.

Rest took a post at the University of Minnesota and developed an objective measure of moral comprehension and preference, the Defining Issues Test (DIT) (Rest 1979b). At Harvard, Colby received a research grant from the National Institute of Child Health and Human Development for a longitudinal analysis of Kohlberg's subjects and to review the scoring manual (Cortese 1986b). The main results of this project were a monograph (Colby et al. 1983), published by the Society for Research in Child Development, and the Standard Form Scoring manual (Colby et al. 1987). Kohlberg (1981b, 1984) also published two monographs, a collection of essays on the philosophy and psychology of moral development.

The history of the school reflects a great deal of research effort in collaboration between Kohlberg and his colleagues (Cortese 1986b). This close working relationship, a true *communitas*, is perhaps the single most important aspect that identifies and justifies the school's approach to the development of the social sciences. Kohlberg's numerous jointly published articles and essays represent the relationship between leader-founder and student that is characteristic of "schools."

In making the case for a sociology of moral judgment, the major point is that society is characterized more by diversity, plurality, conflict, and disorder than by integration and a consensus of moral values. Moreover, we can once again borrow from Durkheim his emphasis on the importance of social constraint to take issue with the notion of autonomous rationality.

The Sociology of Moral Judgment

Kohlberg's theory implies that individual rights are sacred. At Stage 6, in particular, such principles of individualism take precedence over the laws and agreements of one's group or concern for others. By the removal of "constraining" duties, the individual will "progress" toward self-realization and self-expression. It is then assumed that if people are self-principled and have the ability to exercise their individual rights, they will be self-motivated to be good to others. This, of course, does not necessarily follow.

One of Durkheim and Freud's major points is the necessity to restrain and sublimate the natural impulses of the self. More recently, Rushton (1980) has suggested providing models and rewards to encourage people to consider the needs and wishes of others. Kohlberg's assumptions about motivation imply a preoccupation with the self. Yet people can be motivated toward ends other than themselves. The personal problems that draw people to seek therapeutic advice may derive less than is generally supposed from not expressing themselves, fulfilling themselves, or satisfying self needs, and more from not having a feasible way of living in which they participate in applying themselves to the concerns of others (Wallach and Wallach 1983). The social learning paradigm is regaining its appeal, with its much better track record in predicting behavior. The insertion of cognitive elements in social learning models has also strengthened its influence in contemporary social science.

But the competing psychoanalytic and social-learning paradigms also suffer from egoism (Wallach and Wallach 1983). Both use the premise that human beings are exclusively concerned with personal outcomes. What is outside the self has little significance. All three of these schools of psychology lend support to selfishness. Perhaps an alternative paradigmatic can be found in a model that views behavior as being motivated by social interests, a sense of purpose external to the self.

There is also the problem of cultural and social class bias. Why is it that only white, educated, middle- to upper-class males seem to register postconventional scores? In what can be viewed as a methodological split from the school, Rest (1979b) constructed an alternative objective measure of moral judgment to eliminate scoring bias and increase interrater reliability. Rest believes that the individual can and does reason at a range of different stages, not just one basic stage.

Kohlberg's Stage 6 focuses on logical comprehensiveness that promotes autonomy, not connectedness. It sets up moral dilemmas as mathematical equations, ignoring judgment, wisdom, and transcendental creativity. The logic of abstract reasoning falls apart in the dilemmas of real life. The application of clear-cut moral guidelines are irrelevant in multidimensional personal crises. Relativism results from contradictions between abstract moral principles and the ambiguities of real-life situations. Reason and the conception of the moral ideal are stressed by Kohlberg. But an alternative view is the diversity and disorder of experience, the possibility that life itself is unfair. The point is to transcend reason, not ignore it. My pluralistic approach to morality leads to a critical examination of contemporary social psychological models of the self.

In mass society the structure of interaction that results in the development of the self is bureaucratically organized (Young 1980). This is contrary to the position of Kohlberg who argues that high societal complexity results in an autonomously moral self. Yet interactions in bureaucracy and other formal organizations are so brief, so impersonal, and so narrowly focused that the development of a self is difficult. Inasmuch as regulations, commands, and job descriptions mediate behavior in bureaucratically organized societies, the development of a morally conscious self is superfluous. As personal and societal disorganization increases, it has become more pressing to evaluate the current state of social psychology, point out its weaknesses, and construct more accurate models of self and society:

> A society moving toward more fragmented and predatory forms of self needs this self-knowledge more than it needs an army, more than it needs automobiles, more than it needs nuclear-based energy, and more than it needs Monday Night Football (Young 1980: 1).

The structures of a morally inconsistent society needs to be eliminated before an autonomous self is possible.

Morality depends on more than personal judgment. If behavior is mediated by orders, company policy, or advertising psychology, the autonomous moral self is a myth. When one sells one's labor to a factory, retail firm, insurance company, energy enterprise, or president re-election and administration campaign, one sells, at the same time, one's moral character however developed it might be (see Candee 1975). In exchange for wages, one subordinates oneself to the logics of the firm. One must produce what one is hired to produce, whether it be napalm, birth-control pills, or nuclear energy. One must sell on the terms set by the firm, using the sales approach selected by higher authority. Whether those terms are just or whether those ads are sexist is no matter of moral judgment for the clerk. Similarly, a nation's immoral foreign policy is not subject to individual citizens' moral judgment.

"What are the social conditions under which a morally competent self arises?" (Young 1978: 2). The structure of the self is variable, requiring a supportive social matrix if it is to develop, and may not develop at all. The socialization process in the United States is oriented toward the development of skills and techniques sellable on the labor market, not toward the development of autonomy. Similarly, Kohlberg's principled reasoning involves those technical skills necessary to design and control rational-purposive systems. Moral stage theory, which sets this mode of judgment at the top of the scale of moral development, may be more of a political act espousing modern corporate success for individuals.

The concept of surplus population in capital-intensive production refers to people whose labor is not needed and who do not have the resources to buy the forms of life and leisure identified on the mass media as necessary to the "good life" (Young 1978: 6–7). Blacks, Chicanos, and other ethnic minorities are more likely to be surplus population and are denied those identities central to the productive process. Morality, as part of ideological culture, is not produced by situated, interacting individuals (as presumed in cognitive development theory). Rather, it is mass-produced by bureaucratic organization, the media, and technical experts. Ideological culture is produced largely by a political elite, material culture by technology. Consequently, people in the surplus population are excluded from the construction of social knowledge and secondary social institutions. Thus the cultural universality of the cognitive development framework does not hold. "Without jobs or an income, the material base with which to produce a social life-world in concert with a stable set of relevant and significant others is difficult" (Young 1978: 7). One cannot make judgments to obey property laws when one must satisfy physical needs or is lead to satisfy false needs.

Cognitive development theory and symbolic interactionism ignore how the means of production relate to the development and exercise of self. Relations of production are crucial to the structure of culture, consciousness, and self (including moral development). The dialectical relationship between the self and systems of production holds the potential for changing the oppressive character of the relations of production. People forced into menial work by the structures of race, class, or gender privilege may have low self-esteem. This, in turn, may subvert self-control, self-determination, and a view of oneself as a moral agent.

Kohlberg's assumptions represent a general bias in American social psychology that "the self is an autonomous, creating, [and] determining part of the process by which social reality is produced"

(Young 1978: 1). Kohlberg's theory is unconcerned with how individuals relate to the larger society. It assumes equal access to secondary institutions and collective, democratic discourse in policy formation. Participation in societal institutions and in problem solving and role playing are necessary for an individual to develop mature moral judgment. In many instances, lower-class people and ethnic minorities are locked out of this process by dominant groups. General alienation is likely to occur. The rejection of one class of people by another is a group phenomenon, not an individual one. Lower-class people and ethnic minorities fight, adapt to, or withdraw from a society that ignores them, is indifferent to their presence, or is intolerant of their participation. Alienated people often fail to adopt the substantive values of society; they are severed from participating in secondary institutions.

The power to implement innovations is the main distinction between whites and ethnic minorities (Willie 1983). The unique choice for dominants is whether to make the system available to subordinates, so that all can profit from existing resources. No one should gain or lose because of one's arbitrary placement in the social stratification system. The exclusive system, however, has not been transformed into an inclusive one, however; this would entail sharing one's power, privilege, and prerogatives. Kohlberg's highest stage, six, does not address this issue. It is defined as "self-chosen ethical principles appealing to logical comprehensiveness, universality, and consistency" (Kohlberg 1971a: 165). It cannot handle the injustice of real life—and it fails to recognize that a fundamental premise of human reasoning is self-interest.

Throughout the history of moral philosophy, culturally universal standards of ethics have been sought. Such attempts have been intriguing, although vigorously criticized, given the substantial variation of value configurations and related moral positions across time and cultural settings. There has been a recent emphasis on human rights in the academic and political arenas. Human rights imply a hierarchy of ethical standards adequate for moral judgment. One must first determine whether, at a basic level, the concept of morality has the same meaning for all cultures. Most, if not all, languages include a word or term that carries the general connotation of morality, rights, and duty toward others. To be sure, how cultural systems define individual and group responsibilities and rights vary tremendously. Yet our actions seem to reflect at least a vague coordination of perspectives toward both others and self.

The Political Nature of Morality

"Problems, and the directions in which they may be resolved, are posed in philosophy by the evolution of forces of production, by social developments and the development of class struggles" (Lukacs 1980: 3). No philosophy is innocent; it pulls either for or against reason. At the same time it determines the character of its role in social developments. "Reason can never be . . . politically neutral, suspended above social developments. It always mirrors the concrete rationality—or irrationality—of a social situation" (Lukacs 1980: 5). For example, the development of Kant's rationalism was dependent on class struggles in Germany.

One of the most important tasks of moral rationalism was to provide people with philosophical comfort, a semblance of total freedom, the illusion of personal autonomy and of moral and intellectual superiority. But, in fact, reason rendered people absolutely subservient to it. The humanist movement contributed far less to national consciousness in Germany than elsewhere. An important ideological obstacle to democracy in Germany was the ever-increasing, large-scale falsification of Germany history. This rewriting of German history, while ignoring its working class, significantly influenced the methodology of the social sciences. This kind of rationalism turns up again the work of Rawls, Kohlberg, and Habermas.

After attempts to grasp the rational laws of society and history (e.g., Hegel), a fresh wave of irrationalism emerged. German historical theorists battled against the concept of rationally comprehensible progress. The democratic movement in Germany floundered and could not effectively oppose this ideological campaign of falsification. Neo-Kantianism was unable to illuminate the struggles for democratic revolutions. The labor movement's successful struggles to improve their situation and to foresee the overthrow of capitalism led the working class to value rationality and order in their lives, in their own historical development. This "enlightenment" extinguished its own self-consciousness. Knowledge was power, overcoming all obstacles. People paid for the increase in their power with an alienation from that over which they exercised power—their own lives.

Rationality as ideology exalted the self but also acted to cloak one's interest in idealized form and gain deference for proponents of such rationalism. Rationality never sailed under its true colors; there was always a hidden agenda. For example, the bourgeoisie created a new set of ideals: freedom, equality, and "the eternal rights of man"—all abstract universals. Of course, competition for the means of mental production is stacked against the poor, racial ethnic minorities, and women. Formal rationality undercuts substantive rationality. Objects and procedures become more important than people. "As we have become more enlightened and scientifically expert, we have embodied our expertise in massive organizations that no longer think in a human way, but merely follow general principles" (Collins 1985: 95).

Durkheim depicted society as having a superficial conscious level and an unconscious structure within which the real determinants operate. We think that we are rational, masters of our own fate. But rationality is constructed by the social structure in which we live. This structure shepherds us into thinking in one particular way rather than another. Individuals do not recognize that they are determined by the social structure because they are preoccupied with the details of everyday life. One does not simply move about making rational judgments for rewards and punishments, investments and payoffs. Rational moral judgments occur only on the surface level of society. Rational judgment, as Durkheim stated, always has a non-rational basis from which it emerges.

The Morality of Care

In the previous section, I mentioned that a fresh wave of irrationalism emerged in response to emphasis on the rational laws of society (e.g., Hegel and Kant). At the opposite pole from logical positivism, with foci on rationality, logic, empiricism, objectivity, behaviorism, and science lies existentialism, espousing feeling, subjectivity, individualism, and introspection. Martin Heidegger ([1926] 1962), who was strongly influenced by Edmund Husserl, tried to elude rationalism by dealing subjectively with the very content of experience. His starting point was the analysis of *Dasein* ("being" or "being there"). Dasein is temporal or historical, but otherwise indefinable and indescribable. It contains no essence, but expresses only existence. Because people have free will they are indeterminate. Freedom involves self-reflection or consciousness, responsibility, and unfettered decision-making.

The temporality or historicity of people implies that we are more than our present manifestation. We are also our past and our future. Because we are oriented toward the future, to our possibilities, we feel *anxiety* and *care*. Consequently, care is a basic mode of human existence. Care is also an expression of the moral tensions or conflicts that maintain the individual in its grasp in any age and in any society.

The morality of "care" is the main concern of this section. I have used the protocols of my research subjects (Cortese 1984b, 1989b) to illustrate the incompleteness of Kohlberg's theory and method. My main point is that there are other components of morality central for many of my subjects, yet ignored by Kohlberg's approach. My thesis here is that the morality of care is the chief component left out of Kohlberg's system. I argue that the morality of care must be part of any ethical system. There are two aspects to my position. First, care for others is the most fundamental modality of existence (Heidegger [1926] 1962). Second, communication is necessary for care. Within these two aspects—care and communication—lie several themes.

Care

The care component includes caring per se, grief, omission, violence, respect, and narrative style (this last theme was also discussed in Chapter 5).

The Morality of Caring The morality of caring concerns love and responsibility, issues underemphasized in Kohlberg's model. The following concerns were salient to the moral perspectives of the subjects; yet they are typically ignored or devalued in Kohlberg's scoring system:

> **Question:** What do you think is the most important thing a son should be concerned about in his relationship to his father?
> **No. 47:** (black male): Caring.
> **Q.:** Why is that the most important thing?
> **A.:** Because if you know that someone cares about you and loves you, you won't have any problems. You can't always use the excuse, "He didn't love me; he didn't care."
> **Q.:** What do you think the most important thing a father should be concerned about in his relationship to his son?
> **A.:** Letting his son know that he'll always be there.
> **Q.:** Why is that the most important thing?
> **A.:** A son can turn to his father for advice. A father has been through it; a son hasn't been through it. It's like a learning process; a father is like a teacher.

Question: It is against the law for Heinz to steal. Does that make it morally wrong?

No. 56 (black female): No.

Q.: Why not?

A.: For Heinz, the bond when people love each other is stronger than what the court has to say.

Question: How does [punishing people who break the law] apply to how the judge should decide?

No. 16 (Chicana): It's a matter of life and death. The judge, no matter how smart he is, still has to have feelings for people. And, hopefully, he will have feelings for Heinz.

Q.: Should a law-breaker be punished if he is acting out of conscience?

A.: No. Not in this case.

Q.: Why not?

A.: Stealing was the only way for Heinz to get the drug. I can see doing that for a person you love.

Q.: Is the fact that the father promised [Joe he could go to camp if he earned the money] the most important thing in the situation?

A.: It's a big factor for a 14-year-old child, yes.

Q.: Why?

A.: Why? At that age you look up to your parents a lot. For you to break your promise is going to break that kid's heart as well. And then on top of that, to ask him for the money which he worked so hard to earn, it's just unthinkable.

Q.: Is it important to keep a promise?

A.: Promises should come from the heart; to promise a kid something is even more important than promises to anybody else.

Q.: What do you think is the most important thing a father should be concerned about in his relationship to his son?

A.: Make sure that his son grows up right and learns to love himself. And loves other people. And just care.

Q.: Why is that the most important thing?

A.: Because that's what keeps the world going.

The following responses were to the same question:

No. 58 (white female): Care for each other.

No. 30 (black female): Getting along and being able to communicate is all part of love.

While the care and responsibility theme was more common in responses by Chicanos, blacks, and females, a white male also expressed this:

Question: What do you think is the most important thing a son should be concerned about in his relationship to his father?

No. 44: Loving his father.

Q.: Why is that the most important thing?

A.: That's the one thing that I believe takes care of everything else. If you love your father, you'll respect him. If you love him you'll do all the other things that are needed in a father-son relationship. And if you have that love, I believe that carries over all the rest.

Q.: What do you think is the most important thing a father should be concerned about in his relationship to his son?

A.: The same thing—love.

Q.: Why is that the most important thing?

A.: Through that love, you'll discipline, hopefully, in a loving way. You'll teach that son the things he needs to know, and help him; you'll also give him room. You won't be like a dictator—telling him, "I love you so you have to do this and that." You'll also love him enough to know that he can go out and do things on his own—so that he'll be able to learn and grow by himself.

Two Chicanas also stated that love was the most important thing:

Question: Why is that the most important thing?

No. 39: Because love makes the world go around. That's what I was raised on and that's the way I'm going to raise my kids—whether or not we have money.

Q.: What do you think is the most important thing a father should be concerned about in his relationship to his son?

A.: Love and understanding.

Q.: Why is that the most important thing?

A.: Nothing else matters. If you have those things, you'll make it; the relationship will make it.

Question: What do you think is the most important thing a son should be concerned about in his relationship to his father?

No. 25: Love and respect.

Q.: Why is that the most important thing?

A.: People thrive on love; and when you have love and show respect, it comes together.

The following passage combined a care responsibility with role taking:

Question: Should Officer Brown report Heinz for stealing?

No. 33 (white female): No.

Q.: Why not?

A.: Officer Brown might feel the same compassion for his wife as Heinz feels for his wife. If he does feel this compassion, he sees how important it is for Heinz to have his wife survive. He would look and say, "No. I don't think I'll report him."

Q.: Should the judge give Heinz some sentence, or should he suspend the sentence and let him go free?

A.: Suspend the sentence.

Q.: Why?

A.: Hopefully he would be compassionate enough to realize why he [Heinz] had done this and put himself in Heinz's position if he had a wife himself.

Q.: How does [punishing people who break the law] apply to how the judge should decide?

A.: The judge should put himself in Heinz's position. It would be difficult for him—if he didn't have a wife or family—to realize how important it is for Heinz. But the judge should feel human compassion. When he makes the decision he should put himself in that position and not go strictly by the law.

A compassionate role-taking also characterizes this response from a black male:

> **Question:** Should Officer Brown report Heinz for stealing?
> **No. 2:** No. He knows the circumstances and is very personal toward Heinz. He would sympathize with Heinz because that very same thing could happen to him.

Several respondents viewed the Heinz dilemma as involving a morality of care and compassion, not as a conflict between the right to life and the right to property:

> **No. 4** (Chicano male): When it comes to a situation where the law is not being just, I don't think that's right. I would have a hard time dealing with that in my mind. If I did something that was according to the law but yet was hurting someone else, that would be hard for me to do.
> **Question:** What do you think is the most important thing a son should be concerned about in his relationship to his father?
> **No. 49** (black female): Love. Because you need support from your father. Sons and fathers should be close together.
> **Question:** Is it important for people to do everything they can to save another's life?

No. 23 (black female): Yes.
Q.: Why?
A.: It's just something that I feel. If you see someone hurting and you can do something about it, you should lend a hand and help as much as possible.

The Morality of Grief   The second theme is grief. Near the conclusion of an interview, one of my subjects confided in me that his father had recently died. The following response obviously reflected his grief over this personal tragedy:

Question: Should Heinz steal the drug?
No. 35 (white male): If he loves his wife, yes he should.
Q.: Why?
A.: Because she's someone very dear to him. If he doesn't have her, there's no telling what would happen. Life must go on. But I know how difficult it is to go on. And it's not that easy.

This passage illustrates that there is more to moral judgment than issues of justice and conflicts of rights. There is care, grief, and many other affective components that involve a social issue. As the interview concluded, the sorrow over the loss of his father was particularly apparent. The loss of a strong emotional anchor seemed to have a profound effect on the subject's world-view and moral judgment:

Question: What do you think is the most important thing a son should be concerned about in his relationship to his father?
No. 35: Knowing that his father is the role model. Knowing that his father is going to help him. That his father will be there.
Q.: Why is that the most important thing?
A.: For security. It's nice to have someone there. And I know when my dad was there, knowing that he was there, really helped. Because when my dad was there, it made everything okay. I knew that my mom was okay and everything at home was okay. But now that my dad is not there, it makes life tough. Because I don't know what the situation is like.
Q.: What do you think is the most important thing a father should be concerned about in his relationship to his son?
A.: You want your son to know that even through hard times that somebody's being there to help you out.

The Morality of Omission   Not helping someone when you could, and its negative consequences, were mentioned by several subjects:

Question: Should people who break the law be punished?

No. 19 (Chicana): I think people who break the law should be punished if it hurts another person in any way.

Q.: Why?

A.: More and more people are getting away from helping other people. Instead they just try to help themselves. But I don't think Heinz should be punished. I don't see any reason to lock him away for trying to help someone; I just don't.

Q.: Is it important to keep a promise?

No. 17 (black male): Yes. Making a promise usually gives another person hope for something. And breaking a promise usually hurts the other person pretty bad.

Related to omission is the notion that the crux of the Heinz dilemma was the failure of the druggist or the legal system to make the drug available to whoever needs it (also discussed in Chapter 4):

No. 52 (Chicano male): The druggist is trying to cheat him. His wife is dying. He asked the druggist if he could pay part of it now and part of it later. Still the druggist would not consider that. . . . The druggist wasn't being fair to him. If he would have charged less for the drug, Heinz would have been able to buy it; then Heinz wouldn't have had to steal anything. And everything would have been all right.

No. 28 (white female): You wouldn't want to see Heinz's wife die just because the druggist is being selfish. He values his drug more than the life of this woman.

No. 2 (black male): The druggist is morally wrong because he's thinking of his personal gains.

No. 41 (white male): If the druggist won't give Heinz the drug at a cheaper price then he doesn't really have any morals.

No. 32 (Chicana): Heinz's stealing was an act of desperation. The judge should be looking at that awful druggist.

Question: Is it against the law for Heinz to steal? Does that make it morally wrong?

No. 4 (Chicano male): No. I think if anybody is morally wrong, it was the druggist who wouldn't sell it to Heinz.

No. 24 (white male): The druggist doesn't have the right to exploit a person who can't afford to buy the drug. . . . The druggist is too greedy and self-centered to help somebody.

No. 42 (Chicana): The druggist is cheating Heinz.

The following two responses placed the blame on a failure of the legal system:

No. 16 (Chicana): The judge should question the legality of how high the druggist can price his drugs. I think that should be investigated.

No. 58 (white female): There is no right for a law that permits one to charge that much for that drug.

Morality Toward Violence   Some subjects referred to various types of violence in response to moral dilemmas. Men were more likely than women to mention violent behavior in their replies, although several women did refer to violent action. This is consistent with the findings in a study of the images of violence in stories written by college students (Pollak and Gilligan 1982). The study reported statistically significant gender differences in the places where violence is perceived and in the substance of violent fantasies as well. In that study men were more likely than women to express an imagery of violence in stories.

Let us look at some responses in my study (1984b) of those mentioning violence in pursuing moral choices.

Question: How does [punishing people who break the law] apply to how the judge should decide?

No. 36 (black male): In this case, Heinz stole the drug to save his wife who was on her deathbed. It's just like him speeding along the highway to take her to the hospital if she has been shot or stabbed.

Question: Should a law-breaker be punished if he or she is acting out of conscience?

No. 41 (white male): Yeah. Because out of conscience you could rape somebody. And you shouldn't be able to get off for that.

No. 12 (black male): Yes. Because your conscience might tell you to cold-bloodedly murder someone. And if you do that, you should be sentenced for it.

No. 30 (black female): Yes. In some cases people want to murder people. They can say, "My conscience told me to murder you." It's an excuse, basically. But it depends on how valid your excuse is.

No. 52 (Chicano male): If he's acting out of conscience, then there's got to be something wrong with the guy. You can't let him run around if he's a murderer or a psychopathic killer. They should put him in a hospital to make him get back to normal.

No. 60 (white male): It all depends on the situation. Heinz was acting out of conscience. But suppose somebody pissed me off and I got mad and shot him. I was acting on my conscience—shot him in the back, no reason at all. You can't draw a parallel between those two things. It all depends on the situation.

No. 42 (Chicana): It depends on what his conscience is telling him. If his conscience is telling him: Kill that sucker 'cause he's got my woman—that's really stupid.

Question: What do you think is the most important thing a father should be concerned about in his relationship to his son?

No. 31 (Chicana): Guidance and being a strong father figure. I'm not talking gender identity where a son has to see his father being masculine all the time and beating up women just because he'll be macho himself. I don't mean that. A father should share of himself with his son.

The following responses were typical of female subjects, not expressing violence, and seeing the root of the problem in the family or in the environment, not in the actor:

No. 7 (white female): Somebody, at some point, is going to morally judge the criminal's conscience. There's a lot of people who have committed crimes but don't think they've done anything wrong. But they've been judged by psychiatrists and by society in general as being deviant in some way. So I don't think that its a question purely of conscience.

No. 56 (black female): When one is acting out of conscience, it more than likely is a very traumatic or emotional problem or a family problem. There is a personal factor, something that hits home, not something that is going to hurt others or society. I don't think putting him behind bars is the best solution.

Although neither of these women refer to violence, unlike the responses by many males, they can still be contrasted to one another. Subject number 7 answered from a Kohlbergian approach, suggesting societal moral judgments and standards of normality. Subject number 56, on the other hand, paralleled Heidegger and Sartre in emphasizing the basic morality of care. Her response took the personal context into account while number 7 emphasized social prescriptions or roles. This contrast is important because it illuminates two basic, yet opposing, components of morality: the heart and the mind.

Morality of Respect   Respect for elders was a theme which I found particularly in black subjects. It may reflect a value orientation that is more prevalent within particular racial ethnic subcultures. It fits well within the care orientation to morality.

Questions and responses in this section are part of the "Joe Dilemma" (see Appendix, Dilemma I). The story involves an adolescent boy, Joe, whose father promises him that he can go to camp if he saves the money for it himself. But Joe's father breaks his promise, telling Joe to give him the money so that he can spend it on himself. Subjects must decide whether Joe should give his father the money. The dilemma focuses on a conflict between social contract (making and breaking a promise) and authority (obedience to one's father). Subjects are also asked about the importance of keeping promises and the importance of father-son relationships.

>   **Question:** What do you think is the most important thing a son should be concerned about in his relationship to his father?
>
>   **No. 35** (black male): I think that he should respect his father.
>
>   **Q.:** Why is that the most important thing?
>
>   **A.:** A son should respect his father because of the age difference. It's morally right to respect old people. We have been taught not to yell at parents and not to hit old people. No matter how wrong the older people are, you still shouldn't look down on them. Young people have feelings; old people have feelings. The older you get, the more respect you want. You don't want anybody younger than you walking up and hitting you for no reason. You don't want anybody that's younger than you spitting in your face. Older people look for respect in younger people. It is right for younger people to respect older people even if the older people are wrong.
>
>   **Question:** Should Joe refuse to give his father the money?
>
>   **No. 53** (black female): No.
>
>   **Q.:** Why not?
>
>   **A.:** The Bible says, "Honor your parents"—no matter what. If I were in this situation, I would figure something good will come out of it, if you're patient.
>
>   **Question:** What do you think is the most important thing a son should be concerned about in his relationship to his father?
>
>   **No. 23** (black female): To respect him.
>
>   **Q.:** Why?
>
>   **A.:** You should respect all adults.

Communications

The second neglected focus in the research on morality is communication. Many of my subjects viewed communication as the solution for moral dilemmas. Communication involves honesty and trust:

Question: What do you think is the most important thing a son should be concerned about in his relationship to his father?

No. 11 (white female): Communication, honesty.

Q.: Why?

A.: I think it's real important for parent and child to be able to talk openly and be honest with one another. If Joe's father is going to, more or less, lie to him or cheat him out of something he earned, a communication is going to be there and they are not going to have a very sound relationship.

Question: Is it important to keep a promise?

No. 7 (white female): Yes. I think it is important.

Q.: Why?

A.: You have very little besides your own word; I think that your word should mean something to you. In order for it to mean something, it has to mean something to other people too. There has to be shared meaning.

Q.: Is it important to keep a promise to someone you don't know well and probably won't see again?

A.: I think that you should keep your word, no matter what.

Q.: Why?

A.: It's one of the few things that you have that people can believe in. It's something that everyone has. Not everyone has money, but everyone has their own word; I think that they should value that.

Question: What do you think is the most important thing a son should be concerned about in his relationship to his father?

No. 54 (Chicano male): Trying to be open with each other and having some type of communication system open, so that any problems that might come up will be able to be discussed without anybody having any hesitation at all or worry about any reprisals that might happen. If that communication system is left open, even if the son and the father disagree on the solution to a problem, at least it will give the son the opportunity to know the value of being able to express your opinion and have other people listen to it.

Q.: What do you think is the most important thing a father should be concerned about in his relationship to his son?

A.: He should be concerned with spending time with his son, with encouragement with anything he could possibly want to do, and again keeping that communication system open. Plus he should show a lot of love and feeling toward his son.

The subject recounted an autobiographical narrative in response to the question: Why is that the most important thing?

No. 54: It was something my Dad left out with me. He talked to me a lot. He let me express what I felt a lot. But we never really got close to each other—in the way that I feel toward my mother. When I go see my Dad, I don't feel like hugging him. I don't do it. I do hold my brothers and some of my elders; they accept it. But my Dad has never made an attempt to develop that kind of relationship with me. Now I hesitate when I have feelings for him, want to give him a hug, or just spend time with him and tell him how much I care for him. I don't think we ever had the opportunity to do anything like that. I really think that I would have grown a lot closer to him and understood him a lot better.

The machismo of the subject's father—his unexpressiveness and the emotional distance placed between him and his son—is clearly expressed in the preceeding passage. The emotionality of the Chicano culture is also indicated by the subject's closeness to other family members and his desire for closeness with his father. A morality of communication was evident throughout most of the interview, the idea that open communication is the basis for personal relationships and for solving moral dilemmas. Finally, the openness and honesty of the subject as he revealed his regrets about his relationship with his father and views on ideal father-son relationships is noteworthy. This particular passage is important for two reasons. First, it demonstrates the importance of affect and emotion in making moral choices. Second, it also shows how the respondent's real-life relationship with his father reflected a moral choice.

The emphasis on communication was equally evident in an interview with a black male who also expressed regret over an aspect of his relationship with his father:

Question: What do you think is the most important thing a son should be concerned about in his relationship to his father?
No. 15: The ability to relate to one another.
Q.: Why is that the most important thing?
A.: As a son I'm sure that it would be a lot easier for him to find out a lot of things from his father than from someone else. I notice that I found out a lot of things from other people than my father. And that's why, right now, I think it would be a lot easier to find out from your own father.

A white female also noted the importance of communication:

Question: What do you think is the most important thing a son should be concerned about in his relationship to his father?

No. 14: Communication and trust.

Q.: Why is that the most important thing?

A.: Without those two ingredients, you can't have a relationship.

Three other subjects stressed communication in responding to
the same question:

No. 1 (white male): Communication.

No. 38 (Chicana): The communication between him and his
father.

No. 48 (Chicano male): That they can communicate and get
along with each other. And communication involves love between
each other.

Q.: Why is that the most important thing?

No. 1: Communication is primary to anything else in the relationship. If you aren't able to communicate with another person,
you basically will not be able to have a relationship.

No. 38: In order to really know what's going on with each
other, you need communication. If there is no communication then
you really don't know what is happening one way or the other.

No. 48: If they're communicating, they are expressing their
ideas toward each other. There is a strong bond that unites the
father and the son.

In the following interview passage, the subject, a black female,
stressed communication and understanding:

Question: Should Joe refuse to give his father the money?

No. 23: He shouldn't refuse. But he should talk to his father
about it. His father needs to understand the situation—how he
worked to get the money, how his trip to camp was planned before
his father's fishing trip, and how much the trip to camp was
looked forward to.

This subject viewed the process of communication as the solution
for a moral dilemma.

Several of the subjects responded to questions during the interview by asking questions of their own. This is a particular type of
communication. Often the subjects responded with questions as if
to say, "Isn't it obvious?":

Question: Should people try to do everything they can to obey
the law?

No. 30 (black female): Yes. If people didn't obey the law, then what would be the use in having one?

Question: It is against the law for Heinz to steal. Does that make it morally wrong?

No. 39 (Chicana): No. Who says that laws are correct?

Question: Should Heinz steal to save a pet animal?

No. 32 (Chicana): Yes. This pet has been loyal to him for so long. Why shouldn't he steal to keep the dog alive?

Question: Is it important to keep a promise?

No. 46 (Chicana): Yes.

Q.: Why?

A.: Well, why make them?

Trust and Other Concerns

A theme of trust and respect, including self-respect, was indicated in the following responses:

No. 48 (Chicano male): If a father does not respect his son, he cannot expect his son to respect him.

Question: Is it important to keep a promise?

No. 26 (Chicano male): To your kids—yes it is.

Q.: Why?

A.: If your word is worth nothing, then you are worth nothing.

A black male also dealt with trust and respect, but went beyond dyadic and family relationships to generalize about their implications for ethnic relations:

Question: Is it important to keep a promise to someone you don't know well and probably won't see again?

No. 47: I think it is.

Q.: Why?

A.: 'Cause you can develop trust in someone like that. We'll use a white person and a black person, for example. If a black person promises a white person something and the black person breaks it, then the white person is always going to go around thinking that black persons break promises. I think that's important.

It became evident that white males used the same morality of justice that is so highly valued in Kohlberg's approach. The two following subjects formulated the Heinz dilemma as a conflict between rights, as Kohlberg intended:

Question: Should Heinz steal the drug?

No. 1: Yeah. I think Heinz should steal the drug because the value of human life is higher than laws. Laws should not violate the right to maintain human life.

No. 3: Stealing to save a life is not morally wrong. Life comes before a law of society.

Finally, I will touch on ecological validity. I discussed this in some detail in Chapter 4 and gave examples of how some subjects did not respond to some of the questions as posed and provided their own alternatives to the situation. Again, there is a problem for some subjects who were unable or unwilling to relate to the hypothetical nature of the dilemmas. Moral judgments do not occur in a temporal or spatial vacuum. Subjects expressed a need for more detail or viewed the dilemmas as unrealistic:

> **No. 50** (white female): I want to know what happened to Heinz's wife after he stole the drug for her.
>
> **No. 48** (Chicano male): If my father promised me that I could go to camp if I saved the money, I wouldn't have to worry about him asking me for the money later for something he wanted to do. I really can't relate.

Conclusion

The cognitive development approach to morality has spawned a great deal of research and controversy. The research and theories of Piaget and Kohlberg are insightful in elucidating the processes of moral cognition, moral behavior, and the sociology of knowledge. But the theories are limited, not universal. Ethnic groups make their own series of moral judgments, which are sometimes exclusive to their own existential conditions. Social class and gender also mediate moral judgment in individuals. The inequality of social relations is crucial, yet it is ignored in Kohlberg's theory and research methodology. Kohlberg assumes that power is or ought to be irrelevant.

The six stages of moral reasoning are in fact diverse moral philosophies. They "do not line up along some Jacob's ladder ascending to the rational recognition of the inalienable rights of man" (Shweder 1982: 422). To favor any one philosophy (e.g., Stage 6 individual rights over Stage 5 social utility) is merely to voice one's personal or collective preference.

In Kohlberg, there is a paradox between subjectivity and objectivity. Another paradox arises from form versus content. These paradoxes are important because subjectivity can be linked to interpersonal relations, while objectivity can be linked to rules. Similarly, form can represent bureaucratic procedure, while content can represent values and ethical principles. There is a trade-off between rationality and relevance (Shweder 1982); the more rational a moral judgment is, the less relevant it is to interpersonal relations. Awareness of the care, responsibility, and connection orientation (Gilligan 1982) has widened the scope of research on morality, revealing the incompleteness of a formalistic definition of morality. Murphy and Gilligan (1980) discovered stage regression in prescriptive justice reasoning in early adulthood and a change from "post-conventional" morality to a contextually relative morality. Perhaps the last four stages in the sequence need to be reversed.

The development of a morally conscious self is superfluous when the development of the self is bureaucratically organized. Kohlberg's morality fits well with interaction in bureaucracy and other formal organizations. Both involve judgments that are impersonal, formal, and role-oriented. In the context where one submits oneself to the formal logic of the firm or the "universal" principles of collectivities of people, a non-evaluative morality results. It is a "no-sweat" morality; it is easy, mathematical, and void of circumstance and compassion. Stage 6 morality is "just" but vacuous. In the sociology of knowledge, one must recognize that communication plays a key role. Accordingly, there are social conditions which permit, prevent, or retard the development through communication of a morally competent self. In the final analysis, social relations (e.g., ethnicity, race) and social structures are the bases for a moral order.

7

Communication Without Domination: Language and Morality

> Justice and equity, the authority, not of governments, but of conscience within us, will then rule the world.
> —*Immanuel Kant*, Lectures on Ethics

> Morality is higher than human laws. Morality is much more than a group of people arbitrating and constructing what they think is right or wrong. Morality is both individual and cosmic.
> —*Subject Number 57 (white male)*

In this final chapter, I look at how the theory of moral development has developed and been used in contemporary sociological theory. Because moral development theory has supported his critical theory, it has permitted Jurgen Habermas to claim that universalistic, critical thought is grounded in the normal development of the human mind (Alexander 1985; Cortese 1986a). But there are problems for Habermas when he relies on Kohlberg's model. I provide a critical analysis of autonomous rationality, as formulated by Kohlberg and Habermas. I discuss its implications for moral theory and review its development and restructuring from Durkheim to Piaget, Kohlberg, and Habermas.

Habermas has contributed to a more sociological understanding of morality. His institutional frameworks (e.g., "systems" vs. "lifeworld") are essential to understanding the moral theories of Durkheim, Piaget and Kohlberg as sociological theories, not simply social psychologies. Moreover, in opposition to the stage structure of developmental psychologies (Piaget 1960: 13–15; Kohlberg 1984: 215–216), Habermas has offered a structure of institutional/

ideational differentiation and integration. He has claimed that a universal speech ethic is culturally "field-dependent" (Habermas 1979: 93–94). Accordingly, such an ethic goes beyond the context of Piaget's "dilemma" of developing autonomous morality in children through authoritative methods by simultaneously conforming to a speech-community's basic cultural definition of society "as it truly is," i.e., as it *ought* to be. "Ought" is what places the issue in the realm of morality. The ethic espouses the "true interests" and intentions of individual agents, which are themselves defined and analyzed through "the interpretive possibilities of the cultural tradition" (Habermas 1979: 93).

Habermas relies on cognitive development psychology, analytic ego psychology, and symbolic interactionism to develop a type of natural-law ethic of rational dialogue for government as a moral community to compensate for the utilitarian "systems" of the administrative state and economy. Although Piaget and Kohlberg share a strong concern for moral "contracts" between individuals, it is the natural-law ethic assumptions that link Habermas to Durkheim.

Critical Theory and Moral Development

"Critical social theory is faced with the problem of constituting its grounds for critique" (Alexander 1985: 400). Since Habermas's critical theory is explicitly political, its grounds for moral judgment can be explicitly called into question (Cortese 1986a). Piaget's work on cognitive (1952) and moral ([1932] 1965) development and Kohlberg's elaboration (1971a, 1984) of Piagetian moral judgment theory are valuable for Habermas. The biggest contribution of cognitive development theory to critical theory is the assumption that human development is rational and autonomous, not dependent and submissive (Cortese 1986a). Piaget assumed that human intelligence moved from the concrete to the formal, achieving a critical distance from and mastery over relationships among elements of the environment. Habermas (1984) has used Kohlberg to argue that critical rationality occurs in the course of normal development. It is important to note that Kohlberg is less important for his particular model than for the idea that individuals are inherently moral.

In the late 1960s, Kohlberg's Center for Moral Education at Harvard was at the cutting edge of research on moral development and moral education programs. Kohlberg, one of Strauss's students at the University of Chicago, developed a theory in which the cognitive and formal elements of Piaget and the reflexivity of Mead are synthesized. Harold Garfinkel had just published his epistemologically radical *Studies in Ethnomethodology* (1967). An "underground" movement was suddenly thrust into the sociological spotlight. The ethnomethodologists, with epistemological underpinnings in German phenomenology (Husserl [1950] 1960, 1965, [1931] 1965; Schutz 1971) and existential philosophy (Heidegger [1927] 1960; Sartre [1943] 1971), directed the attention of sociology to much more philosophical concerns. But ethnomethodologists were also radical empiricists and provided the basis for a broad critique of mainstream sociology, Marxism, symbolic interactionism, and dramaturgy (Cortese 1986a). Garfinkel concluded that each of these approaches was naive and ungrounded. In ethnomethodology:

> one's own methods of making sense out of experiences are the prime object of investigation. The term "ethnomethodology" itself refers to this focus: "ethno" or "ethnography," the observational study of; "methodology;" the methods that people use to make sense out of experience. (Collins 1985: 210–211)

Similarly, Kohlberg's research methodology requires open-ended questions and allows the interviewer considerable freedom to probe during the Moral Judgment Interview in order to capture the structure of reasoning that emerges spontaneously in individuals in response to standard moral dilemmas. In short, the methodology aims to grasp how subjects make sense out of and resolve moral dilemmas.

Husserl, a major intellectual forefather of ethnomethodology, had renounced all previous epistemologies and set out to establish knowledge on a foundation of absolute certainty. Consequently, he was skeptical of scientific "objectivity" and induction. Husserl termed his phenomenological method *epoche* or "bracketing" (Cortese 1986a). Accordingly, the investigator "takes the contents of consciousness as they come, but suspends judgment as to whether it is true or false. . . . One takes experience not as experience but simply as a pure form of consciousness" (Collins 1985: 208). Husserl argued that these forms of consciousness were universal. Likewise, the search for universal structures of cognition has guided Habermas and Kohlberg.

The convenience of portable cassette players in the late 1960s made possible a new precision for ethnomethodology. "The tape recorder could do the job of capturing every word that was said . . .

every intonation, pause, false start, and all the details that make up actual sounds real-life talk" (Collins 1985: 214). Some of Garfinkel's students, particularly Harvey Sacks and Emanuel Schegloff (both of whom had also been Erving Goffman's graduate students), took advantage of this technology and developed the technique of conversational analysis (Cortese 1986a). Kohlberg also used tape recorders for Moral Judgment Interviews to analyze moral development in individuals.

Ethnomethodology, however, also disparaged the major empirical works of Erving Goffman on everyday life and microinteraction. In microsociology, general questions of epistemology and cognition replaced attention on interaction ritual and the self. Goffman countered the critiques of ethnomethodology, and Blumer's symbolic interactionists with his own "talk analysis" in his last major books, *Frame Analysis* (1974) and *Forms of Talk* (1981). Ethnomethodology was important because it challenged the epistemological foundations of virtually every other major sociological framework. Goffman's works seemed to be singled out for special criticism because while both dramaturgy and ethnomethodology focused on "everyday life," their philosophical assumptions were so opposed that to espouse one seemed to imply repudiation of the other. Habermas, like Garfinkel, Goffman, Noam Chomsky (1954), Claude Lévi-Strauss (1963), and Aaron Cicourel (1973), too became strongly involved with linguistic analysis (Cortese 1986a), and especially the nature of "speech acts."

The next section lays out some of the conceptual intersection between Habermas and Kohlberg. Then the nature of human rationality and the goal of societal emancipation is addressed. A brief outline of the flaws in Kohlberg's perspective highlights the problems in Habermas's borrowing from Kohlberg. We then turn to an examination of how Habermas has used the cognitive development approach to morality in his theories of communication and ego.

Habermas and Kohlberg: Theoretical Intersections

Habermas aims to associate the supremacy of theoretical discourse and practical discourse to the moral reasoning of individuals and to the major stages of social evolution (Giddens 1982). Theoretical discourse focuses on the sustaining of truth claims, involving appeal to empirical observation; it is couched in terms of law-like generalization. Practical discourse focuses on justifying normative claims, appealing to interpretations of values; it is based on moral principles.

According to the models of Habermas, Kohlberg, and Piaget, human consciousness constructs universal, generalizable principles. Kohlberg proposed a structural stage theory for the empirical development of rationality. Habermas ignored Horkheimer and Adorno's (1972) contention that Western cultural development stopped during the Enlightenment, and took on the Hegelian position that the reigning conception of reason was continuing to grow in the course of subsequent Western development (Giddens 1982). Nevertheless, Habermas did not completely agree with Hegel, who viewed rationality as captured in the status quo.

Kohlberg's theory shows how rational autonomy supercedes societal concerns. For example, at Stage 5, with its social contract, utility, individual rights orientation, right consists of an awareness that people hold a variety of values and opinions (Cortese 1986a). Values and rules are typically related to group identification and membership. These relative rules should generally be obeyed, however, in recognizing a need for impartiality and because they are the embodiment of the social contract. But for Kohlberg and Habermas, some non-relative values and rights (e.g., liberty, the dignity of human life) must be valued regardless of societal opinion. Stage 6 provides another example: The right choice is viewed as self-chosen, based on universal ethical principles. Specific laws or social agreements are usually valid since they rest on such principles. If laws oppose these principles, however, one acts in accordance with the principles.

Habermas conceptualizes moral reasoning as a manifestation of ego identity formation. He tried to construct a logic of development and then derive Kohlberg's six stages of moral development from it. For Habermas and Kohlberg, understanding involves communication between the observer and the observed. The method of the social scientist is to "join a conversation." Using Habermas's terminology, interpretation rests on attempting to arrive at a common understanding with another member of the speech community who is uttering a belief about something in the world. In scoring moral judgment protocols, the rater must view the moral dilemmas with the eyes of the subject. "Only to the extent that the interpreter grasps the reasons that allow the author's utterance to appear as rational does he understand what the author could have meant" (Habermas 1983: 257).

There is a conjunction of interactive competence necessary for moral reasoning and ego development. Both Kohlberg and Habermas are proposing an autonomous rationality in individuals, one that would supercede societal rules and convention. For Kohlberg autonomous rationality is necessary for moral maturity. For Habermas interactive competence attained through ego-identity formation is necessary for rational, autonomous morality.

"Cognition," for Kohlberg, implies phenomenological or imaginative role-taking activity, a search for logical or inferential relations and transformations, and the structural level of the subject's meaning. Consequently, moral judgments are indicative of moral meanings and do not describe supposed aspects of the interviewer's mind (e.g., the id). The logic intrinsic to the development of justice reasoning, with the support of the normative criteria of Stage 6, limits the theory as a rational reconstruction. At Stage 6, justice is expressed by the principle of reversibility, of ideal role taking or moral musical chairs. This is equivalent to Habermas's (1979) notion of dialogue interaction governed by a universally recognized speech ethic. Habermas argued that objective and theoretical knowledge constructed from the hermenutic mode rests on theories as rational reconstructions of the implied meanings of individuals' experiences.

Kohlberg (1971a: 223) made a distinction between a normative or moral philosophic theory and an ontogenetic psychological theory: "Science . . . can test whether a philosopher's conception of morality phenomenologically fits the psychological facts. [However] science cannot go on to justify the conception of morality as what morality ought to be." To do so would constitute the "is–ought" fallacy. Psychological data, according to Kohlberg, can provide indirect support for the normative theory, but philosophic or normative grounding is still required because "the empirical truth of ontogenetic sequence does not guarantee validity for the normative conceptions of justice used in rational reconstruction" (Kohlberg 1984: 223).

Kohlberg (1984) viewed the work on "Moral Development and Ego Identity" by Habermas (1975a) as a clarification and extension of moral reasoning theory. Habermas argued that there are structures of communication, self, and society that are hierarchically structured in developmental fashion. Consistent with the cognitive developmental assumption that stages form a culturally invariant sequence, Habermas's theory of communication was supported by the premise that the ontogenesis of communicative competence necessary to engage in "speech-acts" had universal and formal developmental characteristics.

Communicative competence is the ability to successfully engage in speech acts through the mastery of those rules of speech necessary "to fulfill the conditions for a happy employment of sentences in utterances." It develops through three levels of communicative action: (1) incomplete interaction, where the actor is motivated to express and fulfill desires; (2) complete interaction, where the actor is motivated by wanting to understand and follow internalized social norms; and (3) communicative action and discourse, where the actor is motivated by her/his autonomy rather than heteronomy. Communicative competence requires acceptance by the receiver of the message. Thus, three dimensions are involved: external reality, the reality of the speaker, and the shared reality of the speaker and receiver. Just as the ultimate morality for Kohlberg is rational autonomy, so too is it the ideal end point of ego-identity formation for Habermas. Speech acts at the level of communicative action (the highest structure) encourage autonomous realization of self through dependency on interaction with others.

Habermas's theory of communication provided the conceptual underpinnings for his theory of ego development. Habermas linked ego and moral development with interactive competence which involved communicative, cognitive, and social perspective competence. He sought to validate the developmental logic underlying the Kohlberg stage hierarchy. For Habermas (1979: 88), moral reasoning was "the ability to make sure of interactive competence for consciously processing morally relevant conflicts of action." In other words, moral reasoning was a display of ego-identity formation. Habermas thus prescribed and supported a universal speech ethic as the framework for an unrestrained, autonomous ego.

Rationality and Emancipation

Habermas's theory of communicative ethics was an improvement over Kohlberg's theory of moral reasoning in terms of critical political hermeneutics (Reid and Yanarella 1975). Clearly, in highlighting the possibility of social emancipation, in stressing normative values, in offering a macrolevel critique of society, Habermas had made a crucial contribution to the concept of communication (Dasilva 1984). But his vindication of the critical spirit must undergo closer examination. Habermas did not adequately link critique and emancipation (Rasmussen 1975). For Habermas, the highest good was realized through rationality. Nevertheless, critics have pointed out that social action, resulting from the affirmation of the human will, is not always associated with rationality.

Because actors develop a cognitive grasp of the rational course of action, of the right thing to do, it does not necessarily mean that they are going to act rationally. This approach places too much of a burden on reason and fails to grasp the true condition of human nature. Perhaps Hobbes had the clearer insight: humans are motivated into rational action through fear, which is an instinctive, not rational, basis of action. (Dasilva 1984: 22)

The exclusive focus on verbal communication by Habermas precluded non-verbal communication (Dasilva, 1984). Moreover, the rationalistic assumption of Habermas readily became a barrier to understanding human suffering (Heller 1982). There is a gap between rationalism and the sensous world of hope, joy, and suffering in which we live (Dasilva 1984).

Gilligan (1982) has proposed that there is a relational, interpersonal, and responsible orientation to morality (especially by females) that has not received proper attention from Kohlberg, who links morality to rules, principles, and justice. Perhaps Gilligan's biggest contribution is the recognition of an interactive level of morality, mediation between individuals and the social structure. I have pointed out (1984b, 1985) the interaction between the structures of racial and ethnic inequality and individual moral judgment. Similarly, Habermas is intersubjective and recognizes that the level of interaction is social and not at the extreme of subjectivity. Although Habermas and Kohlberg are clearly continuing Piaget's search for an interactional approach to the autonomy-centered model that Durkheim also believed in, they have removed the element of group constraint from their analysis.

From a critical theoretical and phenomenological perspective, the explicit conceptual structure, implicit ideological assumptions, and pedagogical inadequacies of Kohlberg's research can be strongly criticized (Reid and Yanarella 1977). The "culturally invariant" definitions and sequence of moral stages in fact may vary with socioeconomic class (Buck-Morss 1975), racial/ethnic background (Cortese 1984b, 1985), culture (Simpson 1974), and gender (Gilligan 1982). Reid and Yanarella viewed Kohlberg's ideology as an "academic conceit" based on Kantian epistemology and Lockean liberalism.

The cross-cultural data on which Kohlberg bases his assumptions of cultural invariance have been selectively chosen and remain far too limited to support a claim of universal applicability (Simpson, 1974; Snarey, 1985). Fischer (1983) and Phillips and Kelly (1975) argue that Kohlberg and his colleagues have analyzed their data in a rather perfunctory and self-serving manner. Reid and Yanarella (1977: 512) state:

A significant amount of support for the purported sequential structure and universal scope of Kohlberg's moral development scheme springs from the covert role played by the dominant values . . . of Western liberalism. By forgetting the historically specific, socially constructed nature of these values and symbols as they have been institutionalized in our "civilization of work," Kohlberg can forge the "content" of these "forms" of moral reasoning into a hidden universal framework informing the interpretation of the interview data from the national and cross-cultural inquiries.

Kohlberg borrowed Kant's epistemology and characterization of moral principles as categorical imperatives. "As the highest expression of bourgeois liberalism, Kant's thought was a natural object of critical and penetrating scrutiny by critical Marxists from Lukacs to the Frankfurt School" (Reid and Yanarella 1977: 513). Just as the formalism and dualism of Kant can be critiqued as a social product of an historically evolved socioeconomic totality, the fundamental split between form and content that Kohlberg made was especially open to attack. Buck-Morss (1975) maintained that, in regard to morality, form cannot be divorced from content. The conception of morality in terms of justice, responsibility, or rights is not content free.

Kohlberg explained the lack of postconventional moral reasoning in "primitive" cultures and rural societies by reintroducing a doctrine of social evolution which had been refuted in anthropology with the concept of cultural relativity. According to Kohlberg, societies were placed on a continuum from simple to complex. It is in societies where social and political organization was most complex that the highest stages of moral reasoning were to be found. Thus, cultures or subcultures that failed to demonstrate postconventional reasoning were viewed as morally "retarded." To this, Maccoby and Modiano (1966: 269) offered the following response:

The peasant child . . . will experience the uniqueness of events, objects, and people. But as the city child grows older, he may end by exchanging a spontaneous, less alienated relationship to the world for a more sophisticated outlook which concentrates on using, exchanging, or cataloguing. What industrialized urban man gains in an increased ability to formulate, to reason, and to code the ever more numerous bits of complex information he acquires, he may lose in a decreased sensitivity to people and events.

In the same light, the well-documented social cooperative orientation of Mexican and Mexican-American children (e.g., Madsen 1971), though potentially deterimental to their academic achievement, is perhaps more suitable to decision making in an interdependent world of nations than are the autonomous, rational, and competitive modes that characterize the White Anglo-Saxon Protestant model.

A critical hermeneutics of American political culture and society implies that:

> Given the socio-cultural depth of technological rationality in the United States, an instrumental model of reasoning and behavior is an all "too obvious" structure for Americans [and] while none of Kohlberg's research supports it, the experience of fascism in Germany and Italy makes it an open question whether massive regression in what Kohlberg calls moral reasoning . . . but what we would prefer to call psycho-political development—could take place in the United States (Reid and Yanarella 1977: 516).

Keniston (1971) presupposes that without parallel development of compassion, the capacity for love, interpersonal mutuality, and empathy, moral development could result in destructive zealotry rather than real ethicality. Habermas (1975a) states that to the degree that world-views are impoverished, morality too is formalized and detached from substantive interpretation.

Kohlberg seems to accept as given the assumption that what fundamentally matters to each of us is just ourselves, our own self-realization and commitment to autonomous ethical principles. Documented altruistic behavior is typically viewed in terms of positive outcomes for the helping individual (Wallach and Wallach 1983). Such actions are continually traced to the expectation of immediate reciprocity (that one will get something back in return) or at minimum to the idea that the act will make oneself feel good. The portrait of human nature painted by Rawls (1971) is an image of individuals as essentially self-interested and manifesting a restricted sense of good-will.

Wallach and Wallach (1983) provided a comprehensive critique of the subfields of social psychology and developmental psychology for their "sanctioning of selfishness." So Kohlberg is not alone. The strong appeal of Kohlberg was perhaps an overcompensation for the astringency of academic conservatives. At the postconventional level of moral reasoning, we were left with a person "who has differentiated his self from the rules and expectations of others and defines his values in terms of self-chosen principles" (Kohlberg 1976: 33). Kohlberg assumes that the self-chosen principles and motivations of the autonomous self were necessarily ethical. But there is a problem with a morality whereby one's own principles always take precedence over social norms (Wallach and Wallach 1983). This rationalistic perspective has nothing to do with confirmation of the role of morality in promoting the general good or the feelings of others.

Kohlberg supports the desirability of freedom to make one's own choices, independent of the shoulds imposed by anyone else (Wallach and Wallach 1983). Moreover, he assumes that his theory was not value-neutral, but normative or value-relevant. This suggests the more explicit fostering of rational autonomy (Wallach and Wallach 1983). The principled level of morality correlates with the need for self-actualization as declared by Maslow. Both assume that we must respect the needs of self as legitimate. What is evidently most salient for Kohlberg was that the principles of postconventional morality "be the person's own, be expressive of self" (Wallach and Wallach 1983: 194).

Legitimations

Habermas has integrated social science methodology with a critique of science and technology. He is opposed to instrumental rationality as it results in the methodical domination of people. Instrumental rationality emerges within a technocratic consciousness (Habermas [1968] 1970: 111), a type of ideology that makes a "fetish" of science. In short, technocratic consciousness is the "systematic development and application of techniques of problem solving within a routinely bureaucratic context. The technocrat conceives of science and its methods as purely instrumental" (Perdue 1986: 382). In short, technological advance and social change lead to changes in instrumental rationality, which creates new knowledge—knowledge that is often noncritical.

Technocratic consciousness stands in direct contradiction to critical, reflective reasoning. Reason necessitates an examination of the political implications of how and why new knowledge is being used (i.e., to whose advantage and whose disadvantage). Clearly, technocratic consciousness and instrumental rationality are not geared toward resolving the problems of the group or total system. Rather they are used to promote private profit, productivity, and efficiency at the expense of others. As a type of ideology, instrumental rationality permeates the social fabric and is used as a means toward other ends, instead of as an end in itself. Members of society become submissive, unquestioning, and imprudent to the extent that instrumental rationality is accepted. Consequently, it is not possible to be moral; ethics becomes repressed (Habermas [1968] 1970: 112–115).

Habermas uses Weber's concept of "legitimation" to analyze how structures of consciousness uphold established social order. Weber viewed legitimation in terms of authority. Like Weber, Habermas is interested in how people submit to the authority of others. Habermas (1975b) coined the term "legitimation crisis" to refer to how commonly shared justifications for preserving the status quo become more questionable in the wake of exploding contradictions. Governments require loyalty and confidence from their constituents in order to make effective judgments. Yet the types of authority or legitimations run into forceful contradictions found in the often clashing tasks of postindustrial governments. For example, laws must simultaneously support both individual rights and societal welfare. The government supports the individual capitalist when it replies positively to the demands of particular businesses, financial institutions, or economic sectors. It also must play the role of the "total" capitalist and guard the entire system when dissension occurs among its influential parties. Finally, the state should also be responsible for the collective welfare of the general population (e.g., social consumption and social security). In short, the legitimation crisis results from these contradictions inherent in capitalism.

The system of beliefs of postindustrial capitalism produces a mentality of "privatism" in individuals. "The appeal to private interests is manifested in such things as family consumption and leisure, increased career status, and 'civic concern' with little regard for the public good" (Perdue 1986: 384). But Habermas views cultural and structural factors as producing social change that results in legitimation crises. Consequently, such egocentric ideologies are beginning to lose their justifiability and people are more cautious about affirming private concerns. The critique of Kohlberg's theory (and other psychological models) by Wallach and Wallach (1983) parallels this shift in the moral realm. Habermas, like Kohlberg, holds to a vision of the development of a "universal morality." Habermas, however, unlike Kohlberg's focus on self-chosen, individual principles of justice, argues that people will lean toward a more cosmopolitan image of human beings and the nature of human rights. Such a morality creates allegiances that go beyond private and national interests and support the idea of a world community.

Implications for Moral Theory

In tracing the movement of moral theory from Durkheim to Habermas, I have actually been following the ebb and flow of various refractions of the famous object–subject debate which has plagued social scientists and philosophers since at least Kant (Cortese and Mestrovic 1989). Durkheim attempted to find a *via media* in this debate. He labelled his epistemology "renovated rationalism" and self-consciously attempted to avoid objectivism and subjectivism. He seemed to thrive on antinomies of various sorts, including the opposition of formal language to speech, conformity to justice, and constraint to individualism. The accepted picture of Durkheim as a realist and positivist tended to accent the objective aspect of this middle road. This, in turn, resulted in the relative neglect of Durkheim's conceptualizations of language and morality since these phenomena, as we have seen, involve subjectivism to some extent. Piaget accepted the basic Durkheimian doctrine, but was more concerned with the development of autonomy. Kohlberg pushed Piaget's leanings still further by deriving his notion of justice entirely from individualism (i.e., Stage 6). Finally, with Habermas, social theory seems to have reached intersubjectivism. For Habermas, morality is derived from "speech acts" (Cortese 1986a).

Apparently, for Habermas, even Kohlberg is too close to Durkheim's epistemological position. Habermas criticized Kohlberg for neglecting a hypothetical Stage 7:

> Only at the level of a universal ethics of speech can need-interpretations themselves, that is, what each individual thinks he should understand [to] represent his true interests, also become the object of practical discourse: (Kohlberg et al. 1983: 91).

Speech acts are supposed to represent truth, be accurate expressions of the agent's intentions, and conform to the normative context. How can speech do all that? What is to constrain speech from degenerating into what Piaget called egocentric language? The notion of conformity to the normative content harks back to Piaget's dilemma as to whether such conformity is to society as it truly is or as it appears to be, a dilemma rooted in Durkheimian dualism. In short, Habermas's position forces one to reevaluate the alleged progress that has been made in the object–subject debate since Durkheim's time.

Habermas wedded the concepts of language and morality, but at the price of limiting language to that which is speech-oriented, unconstrained, conscious, and intersubjective. I agree with Alexander's (1985: 421) critique of Habermas:

> The "problem" for social theories of modernity, however, is that the arbitrary, unconscious, fused, and, yes, irrational elements of culture have not at the same time disappeared. Language and worldview continue to predefine our understanding of the object world before we even begin to subject it to our conscious rationality. Nor can we regard our linguistically structured worldviews as simply humanly constructed interpretations, which are therefore completely open to criticisms. . . .

However, Alexander did not extend this line of criticism very far; he concluded that we are in fact not faced with a contrast between constraint through institutional coercion on the one hand and complete freedom from constraint on the other (1985: 422). Alexander may be correct. But is that not an echo of Piaget's dilemma with Durkheim, expressed so many years ago? Durkheim referred to a qualitative shift in the kinds of constraints that compel human agents in modern as contrasted to primitive societies, but never abandoned the notion of constraint itself. His claim that there can be no morality without constraint still seems to hold true.

Habermas ([1968] 1970: 92) equates interaction with communication action, which:

> is governed by binding *consensual norms,* which define reciprocal expectations about behavior and which must be understood and recognized by at least two acting subjects. Social norms are enforced through sanctions. Their meaning is objectified in ordinary language communication.

This distinction between the rules conducting purposive-rational action and those directing interactive communicative action is exemplified by the different character of the sanctions involved in each case. Habermas mirrors the distinction Durkheim ([1924] 1974) had made between "moral" sanctions and "utilitarian" (technical) sanctions. Moral sanctions are defined socially; "non-compliance with consensual [moral] norms is sanctioned by the disapproval of, or punishment by, other members of the social community" (Giddens 1982: 104). Utilitarian sanctions are defined by objects and events in nature; "non-compliance with technical [utilitarian] rules or strategies is sanctioned by the likelihood of failure of achieving goals" (Giddens 1982: 104). According to Habermas, rules about purposive-rational action involve the acquisition of skills. Normative rules, on the other hand, involve internalizing personality traits. The account of the evolution of normative frameworks of interaction by Habermas is supported by the premise of correspondence between (subjective) personality and (objective) societal development. In fact, this is the major thread that weaves, in some form, through the moral theories of Durkheim, Piaget, Kohlberg, and Habermas.

Habermas views rationality as an inherent problem and defines interaction as communication without domination. Therefore, he favors a society based on normative symbolic interaction rather than instrumental rational action. The writings of Habermas may be seen as an example of the broader dialectical relationship between subject and object which has guided the thrust of this book. He has carefully indicated that subjective and objective factors cannot be dealt with in isolation from one another (Giddens 1982). For Habermas, knowledge and morality are objective while human interests are subjective.

Habermas seems to reinterpret Piaget as a critical theorist of sorts by focusing on Piaget's understanding of socialization as learning to be rational and autonomous, not dependent and submissive. This is only partly true because, as we have seen, Piaget was not entirely comfortable with depicting this socialization for autonomy as being entirely independent of social constraint. More important, Piaget self-consciously derived this position from Durkheim's theory. Yet many contemporary commentators continue to interpret Durkheim as the advocate *par excellence* of the status quo and submission to normative consensus. I am suggesting that Durkheim's theory of justice has yet to be discussed in a way that comprehends his focus on the reconciliation of social cohesion and individual autonomy, and ultimately, of objectivism and subjectivism. Writing about Durkheim, Fauconnet proposed that "one would not be proposing a paradox by giving [Durkheim's] theory the name of individualism" (see Fox's translation of Durkheim [1922] 1958: 31). Fauconnet may be correct, but his statement seems to be a paradox precisely because the dilemma that bothered Piaget has not yet been fully confronted.

In an unfortunate choice of terminology, Piaget posited a movement from "objective" morality that is really egocentric and subjective to "subjective" morality that is actually impersonal and collective. Nevertheless, the thrust of his developmental theory is strongly sociological and bears the imprint of Durkheim's thought. Subsequent theorists have steadily abandoned the full meaning of Durkheim's position. The result, as I have suggested, is an ill-founded attempt to establish morality on speech acts. There is a need to reexamine Durkheim's notion of justice as depicted by various developmental theorists and to reexamine the sociological import of Piaget's thought. These tasks would be important contributions to Durkheimian scholarship as well as to developmental theory.

Conclusion

I have examined Habermas's use of Kohlberg in his sociological theory. Habermas posited a structural sequence of communication, self, and society that could be hierarchically arranged. Speech acts stimulate autonomous realization of self through dependence on interaction with others. This is paradoxical since the ideal self is using others for self-realization. But the highest morality rests on treating others as ends in themselves (i.e., respect for other human beings as individuals), not a means to justify other ends.

The definition and sequence of moral stages may vary by race, ethnicity, gender, culture, and socioeconomic class. Moral stages, have been incorrectly viewed as having an existence independent of their reified, social construction and their codification by researchers. There is virtually no support for a universality of postconventional moral reasoning in Third World societies. Social action cannot always be related to rationality. In order for communicative interaction to be meaningful, the gap between the technoscientific sphere and the sphere of ordinary human communication must be eliminated. In addition, the fixation on rationalistic explanations of justice omits interpersonal, affective and responsibility dimensions of morality.

Habermas claimed that the development of the ego is universal. This fits well with Piaget's stages since it "makes possible optimal solutions to culturally invariant, recurring problems of action" (Habermas 1979: 70). But although the concept of ego is pancultural, an autonomous ego is not. Habermas believes that an autonomous ego and an emancipated society are necessary partners. Borrowing from Adorno (1973), Habermas (1979: 73) supported the conception of "an ego identity that makes freedom possible without demanding for it the price of unhappiness, violation of one's inner nature." Ego development requires particular cognitive schema but also a competence that results from social interaction. This involves socialization, the process by which individuals learn to become members of society. Socialization is eventually replaced by individuation or autonomy—the end point for Kohlberg and Habermas.

For Habermas, autonomous rationality is the defense for moral action. To be rational, acts must rest on "criticizable validity claims" (Habermas 1984: 15) rather than on sociolegal authority. Kohlberg's model depicts ethical, rational actors who justify their moral judgments on consensual grounds. Right is "justified in relation to a normative context that is legitimate in the sense of reflecting some moral interest common to all concerned" (Alexander 1985: 405). For Habermas, as with Kant, rationality consists of agreement, understanding, and the lack of constraint. Piaget's cognitive development and Kohlberg's moral development armed Habermas with the epistemological grounding that has allowed him to argue that the actor is capable of rethinking the foundation of his/her actions and is no longer subordinate to socially constructed meanings.

A major weakness of Habermas, in my view, is his not acknowledging that there is more to the modern life-world than rationality. Nevertheless, I agree that knowledge based on cultural tradition needs continuous evaluation and critical revision. Even so, reified, arbitrary, unconscious, and irrational components of language, myth, and culture still mold our conceptions of the modern world before we are able to exercise free will, reflexivity, and autonomous rationality. "Modern, rational people continue to infuse values, institutions, and even mundane physical locations with the mystery and awe of the sacred" (Alexander 1985: 421). Furthermore, Habermas's notion that rational communication eventually results in consensus and cooperation is misleading:

> To the extent that cooperation is achieved, it is voluntary only in a very conditional sense. It is always mediated by cultural constraints outside any single actor's conscious control, and for that

matter by institutionally coercive processes that can never be completely superseded. (Alexander 1985: 422).

The structures of ethnic, gender, race, and social class inequality inhibit the attainment of autonomous rationality.

Both Habermas and Kohlberg have dealt only with the cognitive side of ego development, the ability to make moral judgments. But there is more to morality than making judgments. There is also moral action and its effects on individuals and relationships. Similarly, one could argue that people are more important than adherence to abstract, logically comprehensive principles of justice. In the final analysis, the nature of human rationality preempts the possibility of emancipation because it obfuscates essential non-cognitive components of morality such as forgiveness, longsuffering (love's patience), humility, compassion, and gratitude. This is not to undercut the importance of rationality, but to coalesce these with it. Habermas pointed out cognitive components of ego identity which, I would argue, are necessary but not sufficient requirements for human emancipation:

> The actor must be able to understand and to follow individual behavioral expectations of another (level I); he must be able to understand and to follow (or deviate from) reflexive behavioral expectations—roles and norms (level II); finally he must be able to understand and apply reflexive social norms. (Habermas 1979: 86)

Habermas also relied on the crucial differentiation between heteronomy and autonomy as formulated by Piaget. That is, the individual must be able to "see the difference between merely traditional (or imposed) norms and those which are justified in principle" (Habermas 1979: 87). Both Habermas and Kohlberg end with a morality that is totally rational, increasingly abstract, and based on autonomous will. But for human emancipation to occur, one must focus on particular moral conflicts in their context. If morality were merely rational, missing children would simply be statistics. Generalization and rationalization of moral principles obscures the unique biography of individuals. In fact, Habermas argued that in general one person's ego was like all other persons', but as an individual s/he was vastly different from anyone else.

Beyond rational choice lies the motivation to act morally. Too often there is a "discrepancy between our ability to judge and our willingness to act" (Habermas 1979: 92). Habermas recognizes the cognitive–motivational duality of ego development. I would argue that the latter component is as salient as the former. If we can assume this dual nature of the ego, it follows that rationality which prevents total access to any segment of human consciousness also impedes a society's moving toward emancipation.

Habermas clearly reflects his involvement with the Frankfurt School in his critique of bourgeois society. He has written extensively on the role of the state, ideologies, and culture. But he does not adequately relate structural and historical forces to the motivations and consciousness of societal members. Habermas seems to be more involved with the evolution of reason and mind, and for this reason, he leaves out the most important aspects of morality. Apparently, he also does not recognize the recent resurgence of privatism. Technology has made it possible to fulfill leisure aspirations without leaving one's own dwelling (e.g., home entertainment centers). Moreover, new products such as private stereo systems and television sets, complete with connecting earphones, make it possible to turn oneself completely inward. "The motivations attributable to privatism have taken new root. . . . This is an era of *old legitimations in new form*" (Perdue 1986: 385); italics in original).

This, in essence, is a New Social Darwinism that:

> cast[s] nations, groups, and individuals as winners and losers, successes and failures, good and evil. It addresses the problems of chemical-induced distortions (a personal affair), not the distortions of ideology. It projects its artificial systemic self to the whole range of human nature. It promises success to those who hone their supremely *individual* strengths (fitness, fashion, self-help, and self-hype). It offers *private* solutions for public issues. (Perdue 1986: 385, emphasis added).

This new privatism is narcissistic, to be sure, and Habermas's failure to overcome this problem makes him vulnerable to the same type of critique I have furnished against Kohlberg.

Relationships, not reason nor justice, are the essence of life and morality. Conceptions of justice are merely abstract and reified rationality; they remove us from the real world in which we live, and separate us from real people whom we love (Cortese 1989c). Relationships provide the context and the basis for any type of justice, any code of moral principles for which we live. Relationships provide the context for all of our sets of belief, value systems, and behavioral norms. Justice must always refer to some type of relationship; justice is meaningless without its application to relationships. If we do not comprehend the social fabric of our relationships with others, then justice is merely a set of empty mathematical, reified formuli. Justice then hangs dangerously devoid of meaning, like a trapeze artist without a safety net. That is, without relationships justice contains no system of checks and balances. It becomes primary and an end in itself without regard to the purpose of morality. One of the basic reasons for legitimation crises is that we are focused on concepts of authority, law, and justice instead of people, relationships, and life. We are very much aware of the political, scientific, theological, and metaphysical doctrines to which we ourselves subscribe. But we are scarcely conscious of the parallel tenets held by persons of other ethnic, racial, cultural, and religious groups. Consequently, we have the concept of justice, but not justice itself. If we have no deep sense of relationship, we may have a conceptualization of the highest level of justice, but we will not be moral.

APPENDIX

Moral Judgment Interview (Form A)

DILEMMA III: In Europe, a woman was near death from a special kind of cancer. There was one drug that the doctors thought might save her. It was a form of radium that a druggist in the same town had recently discovered. The drug was expensive to make, but the druggist was charging 10 times what the drug cost him to make. He paid $200 for the radium and charged $2,000 for a small dose of the drug. The sick woman's husband, Heinz, went to everyone he knew to borrow the money, but he could only get together about $1000, which is half of what it cost. He told the druggist that his wife was dying and asked him to sell it cheaper or let him pay later. But the druggist said, "No, I discovered the drug and I'm going to make money from it." So Heinz gets desperate and considers breaking into the man's store to steal the drug for his wife.

1. Should Heinz steal the drug?
1a. Why or why not?
2. If Heinz doesn't love his wife, should he steal the drug for her?
2a. Why or why not?
3. Suppose the person dying is not his wife but a stranger. Should Heinz steal the drug for the stranger?
3a. Why or why not?
4. [If you favor stealing the drug for a stranger] Suppose it's a pet animal he loves. Should Heinz steal to save the pet animal?
4a. Why or why not?
5. Is it important for people to do everything they can to save another's life?
5a. Why or why not?
6. It is against the law for Heinz to steal. Does that make it morally wrong?
6a. Why or why not?
7. Should people try to do everything they can to obey the law?
7a. Why or why not?

7b.   How does this apply to what Heinz should do?

DILEMMA III': Heinz did break into the store. He stole the drug and gave it to his wife. In the newspapers the next day, there was an account of the robbery. Mr. Brown, a police officer who knew Heinz, read the account. He remembered seeing Heinz running away from the store and realized that it was Heinz who stole the drug. Mr. Brown wonders whether he should report that Heinz was the robber.

1.   Should Officer Brown report Heinz for stealing?
1a.   Why or why not?
2.   Officer Brown finds and arrests Heinz. Heinz is brought to court, and a jury is selected. The jury's job is to find whether a person is innocent or guilty of committing a crime. The jury finds Heinz guilty. It is up to the judge to determine the sentence. Should the judge give Heinz some sentence, or should he suspend the sentence and let Heinz go free?
2a.   Why?
3.   Thinking in terms of society, should people who break the law be punished?
3a.   Why or why not?
3b.   How does this apply to how the judge should decide?
4.   Heinz was doing what his conscience told him when he stole the drug. Should a lawbreaker be punished if he is acting out of conscience?
4a.   Why or why not?

[Questions 5–10 are designed to elicit the subject's theory of ethics and should be considered optional.]

5.   What does the word conscience mean to you, anyhow? If you were Heinz how would your conscience enter into the decision?
6.   Heinz has to make a moral decision. Should a moral decision be based on one's feeling or on one's thinking and reasoning about right and wrong?
7.   Is Heinz's problem a moral problem? Why or why not?
7a.   In general, what makes something a moral problem or what does the word "moral" mean to you?
8.   If Heinz is going to decide what to do by thinking about what's really right, there must be some answer, some right solution. Is there really some correct solution to moral problems like Heinz's? When people disagree, is everybody's opinion equally right? Why?

9. How do you know when you've come up with a good moral decision? Is there a way of thinking or method by which one can reach a good or adequate decision?
10. Most people believe that thinking and reasoning in science can lead to a correct answer. Is the same thing true in moral decisions or are they different?

DILEMMA I: Joe is a 14-year-old boy who wanted to go to camp very much. His father promised him he could go if he saved up the money for it himself. So Joe worked hard at his paper route and saved up the $40.00 it cost to go to camp, and a little more besides. But just before camp was going to start, his father changed his mind. Some of his friends decided to go on a special fishing trip, and Joe's father was short of the money it would cost. So he told Joe to give him the money he had saved from the paper route. Joe didn't want to give up going to camp, so he thinks of refusing to give his father the money.

1. Should Joe refuse to give his father the money?
1a. Why or why not?
2. Is the fact that Joe earned the money himself the most important thing in the situation?
2a. Why or why not?
3. The father promised Joe he could go to camp if he earned the money. Is the fact that the father promised the most important thing in the situation?
3a. Why or why not?
4. Is it important to keep a promise?
4a. Why or why not?
5. Is it important to keep a promise to someone you don't know well and probably won't see again?
5a. Why or why not?
6. What do you think is the most important thing a son should be concerned about in his relationship to his father?
6a. Why is that the most important thing?
7. What do you think is the most important thing a father should be concerned about in his relationship to his son?
7a. Why is that the most important thing?

SOURCE: Reprinted from Colby et al., 1983.

REFERENCES

Books and Articles

- Adorno, T. W. 1973 *Negative Dialectic* (2nd ed.). New York: Continuum.

- Aiken, H. D. 1962. "The Transcendental Turn in Modern Philosophy: Immanuel Kant." Pp. 235–253 in *The Great Ages of Western Philosophy*, ed. I. Berlin, H. D. Aiken, and M. White. Boston: Houghton Mifflin.

- Alexander, J. 1982. *The Antinomies of Classical Thought: Marx and Durkheim. Theoretical Logic in Sociology*, vol. 2. Berkeley and Los Angeles: University of California Press.

- ———— 1985. "Habermas's New Critical Theory: Its Promise and Problems." *American Journal of Sociology* 91:400–424.

- Anderson, M. S. 1961. *Europe in the Eighteenth Century 1713/1783*. London: Longman.

- Baillot, A. 1927. *Influence de la philosophie de Schopenhauer en France (1860–1900)*. Paris: J. Vrin.

- Baldwin, J. M. 1906. *Social and Ethical Interpretations in Mental Development*. New York: Macmillan.

- Bartz, K., and Levine, E. 1978. "Childbearing by Black Parents: A Description and Comparison to Anglo and Chicano Parents." *Journal of Marriage and the Family*, 40:709–719.

- Batt, H. W. 1974. Guilt, Shame, and the Bureaucratic Model: With Specific Reference to Thai Public Administration. Doctoral dissertation, State University of New York at Albany.

- Beck, L. W. 1969. *Early German Philosophy: Kant and His Predecessors*. Cambridge, MA: Harvard University Press.

- Benhabib, S. 1986. *Critique, Norm, and Utopia: A Study of the Foundations of Critical Theory*. New York: Columbia University Press.

- Benton, C. J., Hernandez, A. C. R, Schmidt, A., Schmitz, M. D., Stone, A. J., and Weiner. 1983. "Is Hostility Linked with Affiliation among Males and with Achievement in Females? A Critique of Pollak and Gilligan." *Journal of Personality and Social Psychology* 45:1167–1171.

- Berkowitz, M., Gibbs, J., and Broughton, J. 1980. "The Relation of Moral Judgment Stage Disparity to Developmental Effects of Peer Dialogues." *Merrill-Palmer Quarterly* 26:341–357.

- Bernstein, B. 1964. "Elaborated and Restricted Codes: Their Social Origins and Some Consequences." *American Anthropologist* 66:55–59.

- Blasi, A. 1980. "Bridging Moral Cognition and Moral Action: A Critical Review of the Literature." *Psychological Bulletin* 88:1–45.

- Blatt, M. Studies on the Effects of Classroom Moral Discussion upon Children's Moral Development. Doctoral dissertation, University of Chicago, 1969.

- Bloom, A. 1987. *The Closing of the American Mind.* New York: Simon & Schuster.

- Bohrnstedt, G. W., and Knoke, D. 1982. *Statistics for Social Data Analysis.* Itasca, IL: Peacock.

- Bouglé, C. 1938. *The French Conception of "Culture Generale" and Its Influence upon Instruction.* New York: Columbia University Press.

- Bronfenbrenner, U. 1970. *Two Worlds of Childhood: U.S. and U.S.S.R.* New York: Russell Sage Foundation.

- Broughton, J. M. 1975. "The Cognitive-Developmental Approach to Morality: A Reply to Kurtines and Greif." *Journal of Moral Education* 8:81–96.

- Brown, R., and Herrnstein, R. J. 1975. *Psychology.* Boston: Little, Brown.

- Buck-Morss, S. 1975. "Socio-economic Bias in Piaget's Theory and Its Implications for Cross-Cultural Studies." *Human Development* 18:35–48.

- Campbell, D. T., and Fiske, D. W. 1959. "Convergent and Discriminant Validation by the Multitrait-Multimethod Matrix." *Psychological Bulletin* 56:81–105.

- Candee, D. 1975. "The Moral Psychology of Watergate." *Journal of Social Issues* 31:183–192.

- Cassirer, E. 1981. *Kant's Life and Thought,* trans. J. Haden. New Haven, CT: Yale University Press.

• Chodorow, N. 1978. *The Reproduction of Mothering*. Berkeley and Los Angeles: University of California Press.

• Chomsky, N. 1964. *Current Issues in Linguistic Theory*. The Hague; Mouton.

• Cicourel, A. 1973. *Cognitive Sociology*. Baltimore: Penguin.

• Colby, A., and Damon, W. 1983. "Listening to a Different Voice: A Review of Gilligan's *In a Different Voice*." *Merrill-Palmer Quarterly* 29:473–481.

• Colby, A., Kohlberg, L., Candee, D., Gibbs, J. C., Hewer, A., Kaufman, K., Power, C., and Speicher-Dubin, B. 1987. *The Measurement of Moral Judgment*. New York: Cambridge University Press.

• ―――― Kohlberg, L., Gibbs, J. C., and Lieberman, M., eds. 1983. *A Longitudinal Study of Moral Judgment*. Monographs of the Society for Research in Child Development 48 (1–2, Serial No. 200).

• Cole, M., Dore, J., Hall, W. S., and Dowley, G. 1977. "Situation and Task in Young Children's Talk." Unpublished manuscript, The Rockefeller University.

• Collins, R. 1985. *Three Sociological Traditions*. New York; Oxford University Press.

• Cook, T. D., and Campbell, D. T. 1979. *Quasi-Experimentation: Design and Analysis Issues for Field Settings*. Boston; Houghton Mifflin.

• Cortese, A. J. 1980. Ethnic Ethics: Subjective Choice and Inference in Chicano and Black Children. Doctoral dissertation, University of Notre Dame.

• ―――― 1982a. "Moral Development in Chicano and Anglo Children." *Hispanic Journal of the Behavioral Sciences* 4:353–366.

• ―――― 1982b. "A Comparative Analysis of Ethnicity and Moral Judgment." *Colorado Association for Chicano Research Review* 1:72–101.

• ―――― 1984a. "Moral Judgment in Chicano, Black, and White Young Adults." *Sociological Focus* 7:189–199.

• ―――― 1984b. "Standard Issue Scoring of Moral Reasoning: A Critique." *Merrill-Palmer Quarterly* 30:227–246.

• ―――― 1985. "The Sociology of Moral Judgment: Social and Ethnic Factors." *Mid-American Review of Sociology* 9:109–124.

• ―――― 1986a. "Habermas and Kohlberg: Morality, Justice, and Rationality." Pp. 141–156 in *Current Perspectives in Social Theory*, vol. 7, ed. J. Wilson and S. McNall. Greenwich, CT: JAI Press.

• —— 1986b. "The Inception, Evolution, and Current State of the Moral Development School of Lawrence Kohlberg." Pp. 327–346 in *Structures of Knowing*, ed. R. Monk. Lanham MD: University Press of America.

• —— 1987. "The Internal Consistency of Moral Reasoning: A Multitrait-Multimethod Analysis." *Journal of Psychology* 121:373–386.

• —— 1989a. "Structural Consistency in Moral Judgement," *British Journal of Social Psychology* 28:279–281.

• —— 1989b. "The Interpersonal Approach to Morality: A Gender and Cultural Analysis." *Journal of Social Psychology* 129:429–442.

• —— 1989c. "Beyond Justice and Legitimation: Interpersonal and Communicative Morality." *New Observations*, Issue 72:20–23.

• —— and Mestrovic, S. G. 1989. "From Durkheim to Habermas: The Role of Language in Moral Theory. *Current Perspectives in Social Theory*, vol. 10, ed. J. Wilson. Greenwich, CT: JAI Press, in press.

• Cowan, P. A., Langer, J., Heavenrich, J., and Nathanson, M. 1969. "Social Learning and Piaget's Cognitive Theory of Moral Development." *Journal of Personality and Social Psychology* 11:261–274.

• Damon, W. 1977. *The Social World of the Child*. San Francisco: Jossey-Bass.

• Dasilva, F. B. 1984. "The Critical Turn on Moral Development: Habermas's Universal Pragmatics and the S. I. Problematic." Paper for meeting of the Western Social Science Association, San Diego, California.

• Davison, M. L. 1979. "The Internal Structure and Psychometric Properties of the Defining Issues Test." Pp. 223–245 in *Development in Judging Moral Issues*, ed. J. Rest. Minneapolis: University of Minnesota Press.

• DeVos, E. 1983. Sociometric Influences on Moral Reasoning: A Structural Developmental Perspective. Doctoral dissertation, Harvard University.

• Dewey, J. [1895] 1964. *On Education: Selected Writings* ed. R. D. Archambault. New York: Modern Library.

• —— and Tufts, J. H. 1908. *Ethics*. New York: Henry Holt.

• Dilthey, W. 1977. *Descriptive Psychology and Historical Understanding*, trans. R. M. Zaner and K. L. Heises. The Hague: Nijhoff.

• —— [1957] 1978. *Dilthey's Philosophy of Existence: Introduction to Welthanschaungslehre*, trans. W. Kluhack and M. Weinbaum. Westport, CT: Greenwood Press.

• Dineen, F. P. 1967. *An Introduction to General Linguistics*. New York: Holt, Rinehart and Winston.

• Doroszewski, W. 1932. "Quelques remarques sur les rapports de la sociologie et de la linguistique: Durkheim et F. de Saussure." *Journal of de Psychologie* 30:82–91.

• Durkheim, E. [1885] 1978. Review of Albert Schaeffle's *Bau und Leben des Sozialen Korpers*. Pp. 93–114 in *Emile Durkheim on Institutional Analysis*, ed. and trans. M. Traugott. Chicago: University of Chicago Press.

• —— [1887] 1976. "La Science positive de la morale en allegmagne." Pp. 267–343 in *Textes*, ed. V. Karady, vol. 1. Paris: Les Editions de Minuit.

• —— [1893] 1933. *The Division of Labor in Society*, trans. George Simpson. New York: The Free Press.

• —— [1897] 1951. *Suicide*. New York: The Free Press.

• —— [1903] 1982. *The Rules of Sociological Method and Selected Texts on Sociology and Its Method*, ed. S. Lukes, trans. W. D. Halls. New York: The Free Press.

• —— [1912] 1965. *The Elementary Forms of Religious Life*, trans. J. Swain. New York: The Free Press.

• —— [1922] 1958. *Education and Sociology*, trans. S. Fox. Glencoe, IL: The Free Press.

• —— [1924] 1974. *Sociology and Philosophy*, trans. D. Pocock. New York: The Free Press.

• —— [1925] 1961. *Moral Education*, trans. E. K. Wilson and H. Schnurer. Glencoe, IL: The Free Press.

• —— [1938] 1977. *The Evolution of Educational Thought* trans. P. Collins. London: Routledge & Kegan Paul.

• —— [1955] 1983. *Pragmatism and Sociology*, trans. J. C. Whitehouse. Cambridge: Cambridge University Press.

• —— 1963. *Incest*, trans. E. Sagarin. ed. L. Stuart Co. This work orignially appeared as la prohibition de l'inceste et ses origines in L'Anneé sociologique, v. 1, 1897.

• ———— and P. Fauconnet. [1903] 1982. "Sociology and the Social Sciences." Pp. 175–208 in *The Rules of Sociological Method and Selected Texts on Sociology and Its Method,* ed. S. Lukes. New York: The Free Press.

• Edwards, C. P. 1975. "Societal Complexity and Moral Development: A Kenyan Study." *Ethos* 3:505–527.

• ———— 1981. "The Comparative Study of the Development of Moral Judgment and Reasoning." Pp. 501–528 in *Handbook of Cross-cultural Human Development,* ed. R. H. Munroe, R. L. Munroe, and B. B. Whiting. New York: Garland.

• ———— 1986. "Cross-Cultural Research on Kohlberg's Stages: The Basis for Consensus." Pp. 419–430. in *Lawrence Kohlberg: Consensus and Controversy,* ed. S. Modgil and C. Modgil. London: Falmer.

• Ellenberger, H. 1970. *The Discovery of the Unconscious.* New York: Basic Books.

• Enright, R., Franklin, C., and Manheim, L. 1980. "Children's Distributive Justice Reasoning: A Standardized and Objective Scale." *Developmental Psychology* 16:193–202.

• Fauconnet, P. 1920. *La responsabilité: étude sociologique.* Paris: Alcan.

• Feagin, J. R. 1967. "Black Women in the American Work Force." Pp. 23–35 in *The Family Life of Black People,* ed. C. V. Willie. Columbus, OH: Merrill.

• Fischer, K. 1983. "Illuminating the Processes of Moral Development; A Commentary." Pp. 97–107 in *A Longitudinal Study of Moral Judgment,* ed. A. Colby, L. Kohlberg, J. C. Gibbs, and M. Lieberman. Monographs of the Society for Research in Child Development, 48 (1–2), Serial No. 200.

• Flew, A. 1985. *Thinking about Social Thinking: The Philosophy of the Social Sciences.* New York: Basil Blackwell.

• Fodor, J. 1981. *Representations.* Cambridge, MA: MIT Press.

• Fuller, B. A. G. [1938] 1955. *A History of Philosophy.* New York: Holt, Rinehart and Winston.

• Garfinkel, H. 1967. *Studies in Ethnomethodology.* Englewood Cliffs, NJ: Prentice-Hall.

• Gernet, L. 1981. *The Anthropology of Ancient Greece.* Baltimore: John Hopkins University Press.

• Gibbs, J. C. 1979. "Kohlberg's Moral Stage Theory: A Piagetian Revision." *Human Development* 22:89–112.

• —— Widaman, K. F., and Colby, A. 1982. "Construction and Validation of a Simplified, Group-Administerable Equivalent to the Moral Judgment Interview." *Child Development* 53:895–910.

• Giddens, A. 1971. "Durkheim's Political Sociology." *The Sociological Review* 19:477–519.

• —— 1979. *Central Problems in Social Theory: Action, Structure, and Contradiction in Social Analysis.* Berkeley and Los Angeles: University of California Press.

• —— 1982. *Profiles and Critiques in Social Theory.* Berkeley and Los Angeles: University of California Press.

• —— 1986. *Durkheim on Politics and the State.* Stanford, CA: Stanford University Press.

• Gilligan, C. 1977. "In a Different Voice: Women's Conceptions of the Self and Morality." *Harvard Educational Review* 47:481–517.

• —— 1982. *In a Different Voice: Psychological Theory and Women's Development.* Cambridge, MA: Harvard University Press.

• —— and Murphy, J. M. 1979. "Development from Adolescence to Adulthood: The Philosopher and the 'Dilemma of the Fact'." Pp. 85–99 in *Intellectual Development beyond Childhood,* ed. D. Kuhn. San Francisco: Jossey-Bass.

• Godel, R. 1969. *A Geneva School Reader in Linguistics.* Bloomington: Indiana University Press.

• Goffman, E. 1974. *Frame Analysis.* New York: Harper and Row.

• —— 1981. *Forms of Talk.* Philadelphia: University of Pennsylvania Press.

• Gordon, M. 1964. *Assimilation in American Life.* New York: Oxford University Press.

• Gorsuch, L., and Barnes, M. 1973. "Stages of Ethical Reasoning and Moral Norms of Carib Youths." *Journal of Cross-Cultural Psychology* 4:283–301.

• Gunzberger, D. W., Wegner, D. M., and Anooshian, L. 1977. "Moral Judgment and Distributive Justice." *Human Development* 20:160–170.

• Guyau, J. M. [1887] 1962. *The Non-Religion of the Future.* New York: Schocken Books.

• Haan, N. 1975. "Hypothetical and Actual Moral Reasoning in a Situation of Civil Disobedience." *Journal of Personality and Social Psychology* 32:255–270.

• ———— 1978. "Two Moralities in Action Contexts: Relationships to Thought, Ego Regulation, and Development." *Journal of Personality and Social Psychology* 36:286–305.

• ———— Smith, M. B., and Block, J. 1968. "Moral Reasoning of Young Adults: Political Social Behavior, Family Background, and Personality Correlates." *Journal of Personality and Social Psychology* 10:185–201.

• Habermas, J. [1968] 1970. *Toward a Rational Society*, trans. J. J. Shapiro. Boston: Beacon.

• ———— 1975a. "Moral Development and Ego Identity." *Telos* 24:41–55.

• ———— 1975b. *Legitimation Crisis*. Boston: Beacon.

• ———— 1979. *Communication and the Evolution of Society*. Boston: Beacon.

• ———— 1983. "Interpretive Social Sciences vs. Hermeneuticism." Pp. 251–269 in *Social Science as Moral Inquiry*, ed. N. Haan, R. Ballah, P. Rabinow, and W. Sullivan. New York: Columbia University Press.

• ———— 1984. *The Theory of Communicative Action*. vol. 1, *Reason and the Rationalization of Society*, trans. T. McCarthy. Boston: Beacon.

• Hall, R. T. 1987. *Emile Durkheim: Ethics and the Sociology of Morals*. Westport, CT: Greenwood Press.

• Hamlyn, D. 1980. *Schopenhauer*. London: Routledge & Kegan Paul.

• Harkness, S., Edwards C. P., and Super, C. S. 1981. "Social Roles and Moral Reasoning: A Case Study in a Rural African Community." *Developmental Psychology* 17:595–603.

• Harsanyi, J. C. 1982. "Morality and the Theory of Rational Behavior." Pp. 39–62 in *Utilitarianism and Beyond*, A. Sen and B. Williams, ed. Cambridge: Cambridge University Press.

• Havighurst, R. J. 1976. "The Relative Importance of Social Class and Ethnicity in Human Development." *Human Development* 19:56–65.

• Hayden, R. 1966. "Spanish Americans of the Southwest." *Welfare in Review* 4:14–25.

• Heidegger, M. [1926] 1962. *Being and Time*, trans. J. Macquirre and E. Robinson New York: Harper & Row.

• Heller, A. 1982. "Habermas and Marxism." Pp. 21–41 in *Habermas: Critical Debates*, ed. J. B. Thompson and D. Held. Cambridge, MA: MIT Press.

• Holborn, H. 1968. *A History of Modern Germany 1648–1840*. New York: Alfred A. Knopf.

• Hobhouse, L. T. 1906. *Morals in Evolution: A Study in Comparative Ethics*. London: Chapman and Hall.

• Holstein, C. 1976. "Development of Moral Judgment: A Longitudinal Study of Males and Females." *Child Development* 47:51–61.

• Horkheimer, M., and Adorno, T. W. 1972. *Dialectic of Enlightenment*, trans. J. Cumming. New York: Herder and Herder.

• Husserl, E. [1950] 1960. *Cartesian Meditations*, trans. D. Cairns. The Hague: Nijhoff.

• ——— 1965. *Phenomenology and the Crisis of Philosophy*, trans. Q. Lauer. New York: Harper and Row.

• ——— [1931] 1975. *Ideas: General Introduction to Pure Phenomenology*, trans. W. R. Boyce Gibson. New York: Macmillan.

• Issacs, S. 1966. *Intellectual Growth in Young Children* (2nd ed.). New York: Schocken.

• Janik, A., and Toulmin, S. 1973. *Wittgenstein's Vienna*. New York: Simon & Schuster.

• Jencks, C. 1972. *Inequality*. New York: Basic Books.

• Jensen, A. R. 1969. "How Much Can We Boost IQ and Scholastic Achievement?" *Harvard Educational Review* 39:1–123.

• Johnson, N. J., and Sanday, P. R. 1971. "Subcultural Variations in One Urban Poor Population." *American Anthropology* 73:128–142.

• Joreskog, K. C., and Sorbom, D. 1983. *LISREL: Analysis of Linear Structural Relationships by the Method of Maximum Likelihood*. Chicago: International Educational Services.

• Kant, I. [1781] 1950. *Immanuel Kant's Critique of Pure Reason*, trans. N. K. Smith. New York: Humanities Press.

• ——— [1788] 1949. *Critique of Practical Reason and Other Writings in Moral Philosophy*, trans. and ed. L. W. Beck. Chicago: University of Chicago Press.

• ——— 1963. *Lectures on Ethics*, trans. L. Infield, ed. L. W. Beck. New York: Harper & Row.

• Keniston, K. 1971. "Idealists: The Perils of Principle." Pp. 251–268 in *Youth and Dissent: The Rise of the New Opposition* K. Keniston. New York: Harcourt Brace Jovanovich.

- Kerber, L. K., Greeno, C. G., Maccoby, E. E., Luria, Z., Stack, C. B., and Gilligan, C. 1986. *"In a Different Voice:* An Interdisciplinary Forum." *Signs: Journal of Women in Culture and Society* 11:304–333.

- Kim, J., and Mueller, C. 1978. *Introduction to Factor Analysis: What it is and How to do it.* Sage University Paper series on Quantitative Applications in the Social Sciences, series no. 07–013. Beverly Hills and London: Sage Publications.

- Kohlberg, L. 1958. The Development of Modes of Moral Thinking and Choice in the Years Ten to Sixteen. Doctoral dissertation, University of Chicago.

- ———— 1963. "The Development of Children's Orientation toward a Moral Order: Sequence in the Development of Moral Thought." *Vita Humana* 6:11–33.

- ———— 1966. "Cognitive Stages and Preschool Education." *Human Development* 9:5–17.

- ———— 1969. "Stage and Sequence: The Cognitive-Developmental Approach to Socialization." Pp. 347–480 in *Handbook of Socialization Theory and Research,* ed. D. A. Goslin. Chicago: Rand McNally.

- ———— 1970. "Education for Justice: A Modern Statement of the Platonic View." Pp. 57–83 in *Moral Education,* ed. T. Sizer. Cambridge, MA: Harvard University Press.

- ———— 1971a. "From Is to Ought: How to Commit the Naturalistic Fallacy and Get Away with It in the Study of Moral Development." Pp. 151–235 in *Cognitive Development and Epistemology,* ed. T. Michel. New York: Academic Press.

- ———— 1971b. "Stages of Moral Development as a Basis for Moral Education. Pp. 23–92 in *Moral Education: Interdisciplinary Approaches,* ed. C. Beck, B. Crittenden, and E. Sullivan. Toronto: University of Toronto Press.

- ———— 1973. "Continuities in Childhood and Adult Moral Development Revisited." Pp. 179–204 in *Life-span Developmental Psychology: Personality and Socialization,* ed. P. B. Baltes and K. W. Schaise. New York: Academic Press.

- ———— 1976. "Moral Stages and Moralization: The Cognitive-Developmental Approach." Pp. 31–53 in *Moral Development and Behavior,* ed. T. Lickona. New York: Holt, Rinehart and Winston.

- ———— 1979. "Forward." Pp. vii–xvi in *Development in Judging Moral IIssues,* ed. J. Rest. Minneapolis: University of Minnesota Press.

• —— 1981a. *The Meaning and Measurement of Moral Development.* Heinz Werner Memorial Lecture Series, No. 13. Worcester, MA: Clark University Press.

• —— 1981b. *Essays in Moral Development:* vol. I, *The Philosophy of Moral Development.* New York: Harper & Row.

• —— 1984. *Essays in Moral Development:* vol. II, *The Psychology of Moral Development.* New York: Harper & Row.

• —— and Candee, D. 1984. "Relationship of Moral Judgment to Moral Action. Pp. 498–581 in *Essays in Moral Development:* vol. II, *The Psychology of Moral Development,* ed. L. Kohlberg. New York: Harper & Row.

• —— and Colby, A. 1983. "Reply to Fischer and Saltzstein." Pp. 120–124 in *A Longitudinal Study of Moral Judgment,* ed. A. Colby, L. Kohlberg, J. Gibbs, and M. Lieberman. Monographs of the Society for Research in Child Development 48 (1–2), Serial No. 200.

• —— Colby, A., Gibbs, J. C., Speicher-Dubin, B., and Powers, C. 1978. *Assessing Moral Development Stages: A Manual.* Cambridge, MA: Center for Moral Education, Harvard University.

• —— and Kramer, R. 1969. "Continuities and Discontinuities in Children and Adult Moral Development." *Human Development* 12:13–20.

• —— Levin, C. and Hewer, A. 1983. *Moral Stages: A Current Formulation and a Response to Critics.* Basel: Karger.

• —— Snarey, J., and Reimer, J. 1984. "Cultural Universality in Moral Judgment Stages: A Longitudinal Study in Israel." Pp. 594–620 in *Essays in Moral Development:* vol. II, *The Psychology of Moral Development,* ed. L. Kohlberg. New York: Harper & Row.

• Kohn, M. L. 1963. "Social Class and Parent-Child Relationships." *American Journal of Sociology* 68:471–480.

• Kramer, R. 1968. Moral Development in Young Adulthood. Doctoral dissertation, University of Chicago.

• Krebs, D., and Rosenwald, A. 1977. "Moral Reasoning and Moral Behavior in Conventional Adults." *Merrill-Palmer Quarterly* 23:77–87.

• Krebs, R. L. 1967. Some Relationships between Moral Judgment, Attention and Resistance to Temptation. Doctoral dissertation, University of Chicago.

• Kuhn, D. 1976. "Short-Term Longitudinal Evidence for the Sequentiality of Kohlberg's Early Stages of Moral Judgment." *Developmental Psychology* 12:162–166.

- Kurtines, W., and Greif, E. G. 1974. "The Development of Moral Thought. Review and Evaluation of Kohlberg's Approach." *Psychological Bulletin* 81:453–470.

- ———— and Pimm, J. B. 1983. "The Moral Development Scale: A Piagetian Measure of Moral Judgment." *Educational and Psychological Measurement* 43:89–105.

- Lalande, A. [1926] 1980. *Vocabulaire technique et critique de la philosophie.* Paris: Presses Universitaires de France.

- Lei, T. and Chung, S. 1984. "An Empirical Study of Kohlberg's Theory and Scoring System of Moral Judgment in Chinese Society." Unpublished manuscript, Center for Moral Education, Harvard University, Cambridge, MA.

- Lerner, R. M. 1976. *Concepts and Theories of Human Development.* Reading, MA: Addison-Wesley.

- Lévi-Strauss, C. 1962. *The Savage Mind,* trans. G. Weidenfeld. Chicago: University of Chicago Press.

- ———— 1963. *Structural Anthropology,* trans. C. Jacobson and B. G. Schoepf. New York: Basic Books.

- Levy-Bruhl, L. 1899. *The History of Modern Philosophy in France.* Chicago: Open Court Publishing.

- Logue, W. 1983. *From Philosophy to Sociology: The Evolution of French Liberalism, 1870–1914.* De Kalb, IL: Northern Illinois University Press.

- Lukacs, G. 1980. *The Destruction of Reason,* trans. P. Palmer. London: Merlin.

- Maccoby, M., and Modiano, N. 1966. "On Culture and Equivalence." Pp. 257–269 in *Studies in Cognitive Growth,* ed. J. Bruner, R. Olver, and P. Greenfield. New York: Wiley.

- MacIntyre, A. 1982. *After Virtue.* Notre Dame, IN: University of Notre Dame Press.

- Madsen, M. C. 1971. "Developmental and Cross-Cultural Differences in the Cooperative and Competitive Behavior of Young Children." *Journal of Cross-Cultural Psychology* 4:365–371.

- Magee, B. 1983. *The Philosophy of Schopenhauer.* New York: Oxford University Press.

- Mangan, J. 1978. "Piaget's Theory and Cultural Differences." *Human Development* 21:170–189.

- Mann, T. [1939] 1955. "Introduction." Pp. iii–xxiii in *The Works of Schopenhauer,* ed. W. Durant and T. Mann. New York: Frederick Ungar.

- Mannheim, K. [1936] 1971. *Ideology and Utopia,* trans. L. Worth and E. Shils. New York: Hartcourt, Brace, and World.

- ——— 1967. *Men and Society in an age of Reconstruction,* trans. E. Shils. New York: Hartcourt, Brace and World.

- Marx, K. [1884] 1961. *Economic and Philosophic Manuscripts of 1844.* Moscow: Foreign Languages Publishing House.

- ——— [1857–1858] 1971. *The Grundrisse,* ed. and trans. D. McLellen. New York: International Publishers.

- ——— [1867–1895] 1967. *Capital: A Critique of Political Economy.* 3 vols. New York: International Publishers.

- Mauro, T. [1967] 1978. "Notes biographiques et critiques sur Ferdinand de Saussure." Pp. 319–389 in *Cours de linguistique generale.* Paris: Payot.

- Mauss, M. [1950] 1979. *Sociology and Psychology.* London: Routledge & Kegan Paul.

- McDougall, W. 1908. *An Introduction to Social Psychology.* London: Methuen.

- Mead, G. H. 1934. *Mind, Self, and Society.* Chicago: University of Chicago Press.

- Meillet, A. 1982. *Linguistique historique et linguistique générale.* Paris: Champion.

- Merton, R. [1949] 1968. *Social Theory and Social Action* (3rd ed.). New York: The Free Press.

- Mestrovic, S. G. 1985. "Durkheim's Renovated Rationalism and the Idea That 'Collective Life Is Only Made of Representation.'" *Current Perspectives in Social Theory* 6:199–218.

- Milgram, S. 1974. *Obedience to Authority.* New York: Harper & Row.

- Moir, J. 1974. "Egocentrism and the Emergence of Conventional Morality in Preadolescent Girls." *Child Development* 45:299–304.

- Mounin, G. 1975. *La linguistique du XXe siècle.* Paris: Presses Universitaires de France.

- Murphy, J. M., and Gilligan, C. 1980. "Moral Development in Late Adolescence and Adulthood: A Critique and Reconstruction of Kohlberg's Theory." *Human Development* 23:77–104.

- Murrillo, N. 1971. "The Mexican-American Family." Pp. 97–108 in *Chicanos: Social and Psychological Perspectives* (2nd ed.) ed. C. A. Hernandez, M. J. Haug, N. N. Wagner. St. Louis: C. V. Mosby Press.

- Nicolayev, J., and Phillips, D. C. 1978. "Kohlbergian Moral Development: A Progressing or Degenerating Research Program?" *Educational Theory* 28:286–301.

- Nisan, M., and Kohlberg, L. 1982. "Universality and Variation in Moral Judgment: A Longitudinal and Cross-Sectional Study in Turkey." *Child Development* 53:865–876.

- Nisbet, R. A. 1974. *The Sociology of Emile Durkheim.* New York: Oxford University Press.

- Parikh, B. 1975. Moral Judgment and Development and Its Relation to Family Environmental Factors in Indian and American Urban Upper-Middle-Class Families. Doctoral dissertation, Boston University.

- Parsons, T. 1951. *The Social System.* Glencoe, IL: The Free Press.

- ———— [1949] 1968. *The Structure of Social Action.* New York: The Free Press.

- Penalosa, F., and McDonagh, E. C. 1966. "Social Mobility in a Mexican-American Community." *Social Forces* 44:498–505.

- Perdue, W. D. 1986. *Sociological Theory.* Palo Alto, CA: Mayfield.

- Phillips, D. C., and Kelly, M. 1975. "Hierarchical Theories of Development in Education and Psychology." *Harvard Educational Review* 45:366–367.

- Piaget, 1926. *The Language and Thought of the Child,* trans. M. and R. Gabain. London: Routledge & Kegan Paul.

- ———— [1932] 1965. *The Moral Judgment of the Child* (2nd ed.). New York: The Free Press.

- ———— 1951. *Play, Dreams and Imitation in Childhood.* New York: Norton.

- ———— 1952. *The Origins of Intelligence in Children.* London: Routledge & Kegan Paul.

- ———— 1953. *Logic and Psychology.* Manchester: Manchester University Press.

- ———— 1954. *The Construction of Reality.* New York: Basic Books.

- ———— 1960. "The General Problems of the Psychobiological Development of the Child." Pp. 3–27 in *Discussion on Child Development:*

Proceedings of the World Health Organization Study Group on the Psychobiological Development of the Child, vol. 4, ed. J. M. Tanner and B. Inhelder. New York: International Universities Press.

• —— [1955] 1966. *The Language and Thought of the Child.* New York: World.

• —— 1969. *The Mechanism of Perception.* London: Routledge & Kegan Paul.

• —— and Inhelder, B. 1969. *The Psychology of the Child.* New York: Basic Books.

• Pollak, S., and Gilligan, C. 1982. "Images of Violence in Thematic Apperception Test Stories." *Journal of Personality and Social Psychology* 42:159–167.

• Rasmussen, D. 1975. "The Symbolism of Marx: From Alienation to Fetishism." *Cultural Hermeneutics* 3:41–55.

• Rawls, J. 1971. *A Theory of Justice.* Cambridge, MA: Harvard University Press.

• Redfield, R. 1956. *Peasant Society and Culture.* Chicago: University of Chicago Press.

• —— 1962. *Human Nature and the Study of Society: The Collected Papers of Robert Redfield.* Chicago: University of Chicago Press.

• Reid, H. G., and Yanarella, E. J. 1977. "Critical Political Theory and Moral Development: On Kohlberg, Hampden-Turner, and Habermas," *Theory and Society* 4:505–541.

• Rest, J. 1969. Hierarchies of Comprehension and Preference in a Developmental Stage Model of Moral Thinking. Doctoral dissertation, University of Chicago.

• —— 1979a. *Development in Judging Moral Issues.* Minneapolis: University of Minnesota Press.

• —— 1979b. *Revised Manual for the Defining Issues Test: An Objective Test of Moral Judgment Development.* Minneapolis: Minnesota Moral Research Projects, University of Minnesota.

• —— 1983. "Morality." Pp. 556–629 in *Handbook of Child Psychology:* vol. 3. *Cognitive Development,* ed. J. H. Flavell and E. Markman (4th ed.) New York: Wiley.

• —— Turiel, E., and Kohlberg, L. 1969. "Level of Moral Development as a Determinant of Preference and Comprehension of Moral Judgments Made by Others." *Journal of Personality* 37:225–252.

- Rushton, J. 1980. *Altruism, Socialization, and Society.* Englewood Cliffs, NJ: Prentice-Hall.

- Sartre, J. P. [1943] 1971. *Being and Nothingness.* New York: Washington Square Press.

- Saussure, F. [1916] 1959. *Course in General Linguistics,* trans. W. Baskin. New York: Philosophical Library.

- Schlucter, W. 1981. *The Rise of Western Rationalism: Max Weber's Developmental History,* trans. and intro. G. Roth. Berkeley and Los Angeles: University of California Press.

- Schopenhauer, A. [1818] 1977. *The World as Will and Idea.* 3 vols. New York: AMS Press.

- Schutz, A. 1971. *Collected Papers,* vol. 1, ed. and intro. M. Natanson. The Hague: Nijhoff.

- Shweder, R. 1982. "Liberalism as Destiny: Review of Lawrence Kohlberg's *Essays in Moral Development:* vol. I, *The Philosophy of Moral Development.*" *Contemporary Psychology* 27:421–424.

- Siegal, M. 1980. "Kohlberg versus Piaget: To What Extent Has One Theory Eclipsed the Other?" *Merrill-Palmer Quarterly* 26:285–297.

- Simmel, G. [1907] 1987. *Schopenhauer and Nietzsche.* Amherst: University of Massachusetts Press.

- Simpson, A., and Graham, D. 1971. "The Development of Moral Judgment, Emotion, and Behavior in British Adolescents." Unpublished manuscript, University of Durham, Durham, England.

- Simpson, E. L. 1974. "Moral Development Research: A Case Study of Scientific Cultural Bias." *Human Development* 17:81–106.

- Snarey, J. 1982. The Social and Moral Development of Kibbutz Founders and Sabras: A Longitudinal and Cross-Sectional Cross-Cultural Study. Doctoral dissertation, Harvard University.

- ———. 1985. "Cross-Cultural Universality of Social-Moral Development: A Critical Review of Kohlbergian Research." *Psychological Bulletin* 97:202–232.

- ——— Reimer, J., and Kohlberg, L. 1985. "The Development of Social-Moral Reasoning among Kibbutz Adolescents: A Longitudinal Cross-Cultural Study." *Developmental Psychology* 21:3–17.

- Spencer, H. 1899. *The Principles of Ethics,* vol. I. New York: D. Appleton.

• Stang, D. J., and Wrightsman, L. S. 1981. *Dictionary of Social Behavior and Social Research Methods*. Monterey, CA: Brooks/Cole.

• Strikwerda, R. A. 1982. Emile Durkheim's Philosophy of Science: Framework for a New Social Science. Doctoral dissertation, University of Notre Dame.

• Sullivan, E., Beck, C., Joy, M., and Pagliuso, S. 1975. *Moral Learning: Some Findings, Issues and Questions*. Paramus, NJ: Paulist Press.

• —— 1977. "A Study of Kohlberg's Structural Theory of Moral Development". "A Critique of Liberal Social Science Ideology." *Human Development* 20:352–376.

• Tarde, J. G. de. [1903] 1962. *The Laws of Imitation*, trans. and ed. E. C. Parsons. Gloucester, MA: P. Smith.

• —— 1969. *On Communication and Social Influence*, ed. T. N. Clark. Chicago: University of Chicago Press.

• Taylor, R. 1985. *Ethics, Faith, and Reason*. Englewood Cliffs, NJ: Prentice-Hall.

• Tietjen, A., and Walker L. 1984. "Moral Reasoning and Leadership among Men in a Papau New Guinea Village." Unpublished manuscript, University of British Columbia, Vancouver, Canada.

• Tiryakian, E. 1979. "The Significance of Schools in the Development of Sociology." Pp. 211–233 in *Contemporary Issues in Theory and Research: A Metasociological Perspective*, ed. W. E. Snizek, E. R. Furman, and M. K. Miller. Westport, CN: Greenwood.

• Toennies, F. [1887] 1963. *Community and Society*, trans. and ed. C. P. Loomis. New York: Harper & Row.

• Trainer, F. E. 1977. "A Critical Analysis of Kohlberg's Theory." *Journal for the Theory of Social Behavior* 71:41–63.

• Traugott, M. 1978. *Emile Durkheim on Institutional Analysis*. Chicago: University of Chicago Press.

• Trigg, R. 1985. *Understanding Social Science*. New York: Basil Blackwell.

• Turiel, E. 1965. An Experimental Test of the Sequentiality of Developmental Stages in the Child's Moral Judgments. Doctoral dissertation, Yale University.

• —— 1966. "An Experimental Test of the Sequentiality of Developmental Stages in the Child's Moral Judgments." *Journal of Personality and Social Psychology* 3:611–618.

• ———— 1969. "Developmental Processes in the Child's Moral Thinking." Pp. 92–113 in *Trends and Issues in Developmental Psychology*, ed. P. Mussen, J. Langer, and M. Covington. New York: Holt, Rinehart and Winston.

• ———— 1972. "Stage Transition in Moral Development." Pp. 732–758 in *Second Handbook of Research on Teaching*, ed. R. M. Travers. Chicago: Rand McNally.

• ———— 1978. "Social Regulations and Domains of Social Concepts." Pp. 45–74 in *New Directions for Development: Social Cognition*, ed. W. Damon. San Francisco: Jossey-Bass.

• ———— Edwards, C. P., and Kohlberg, L. 1978. "Moral Development in Turkish Children, Adolescents, and Young Adults." *Journal of Cross-Cultural Psychology* 9:75–86.

• ———— and Rothman, G. R. 1972. "The Influence of Reasoning on Behavioral Choices at Different Stages of Moral Development." *Child Development* 43:741–756.

• Ulibarri, H. 1966. "Social and Attitudinal Characteristics of Spanish-Speaking Migrant and Ex-Migrant Workers in the Southwest." *Sociology and Social Research* 50:361–370.

• U.S. Labor Department. 1965. *The Negro Family, A Case for National Action*. Washington, D.C.: Government Printing Office.

• Vanderburg, W. H. 1985. *The Growth of Minds and Cultures*. Toronto: University of Toronto Press.

• Vasudev, J. 1983. "A Study of Moral Reasoning at Different Life Stages in India." Unpublished manuscript, University of Pittsburgh, Pittsburgh, PA.

• Vendryes, J. 1921. "Le caractère social du language et la doctrine de Ferdinand de Saussure." *Journal de Psychologie* 18:617–624.

• Vygotsky, L. S. 1935. *Mental Development in the Process of Education*. Moscow and Leningrad: State Pedogogical Publishing House.

• Walker, L. 1984. "Sex Differences in the Development of Moral Reasoning: A Critical Review of the Literature." *Child Development* 55:677–691.

• Wallach, M. A., and Wallach, L. 1983. *Psychology's Sanction for Selfishness*. San Francisco: W. H. Freeman.

• White, B. 1974. "Moral Development in Bahamian School Children: A Cross-Cultural Examination of Kohlberg's Stages of Moral Reasoning." *Developmental Psychology* 11:535–536.

• White, C. B., Bushnell, N., and Regnemer, J. L. 1978. "Moral Development in Bahamian School Children: A 3-Year Examination of Kohlberg's Stages of Moral Development." *Developmental Psychology* 14: 58–65.

• Willie, C. V., ed. 1979. *The Caste and Class Controversy.* Bayside, NY: General Hall.

• ———— 1983. *Race, Ethnicity, and Socioeconomic Status.* Bayside, NY: General Hall.

• Wilson, W. J. 1979. *The Declining Significance of Race.* Chicago: University of Chicago Press.

• Wundt, W. 1907. *The Principles of Morality and the Departments of the Moral Life.* New York: Macmillan.

• Young, T. R. 1978. "Some Theses on the Structure of the Self." Paper for Third Annual Conference on the Current State of Marxist Theory, October.

• ———— 1980. "The Structure of Self in Mass Society: Against Zurcher." Transforming Sociology Series, The Red Feather Institute. Red Feather Lakes, Colorado.

• Yussen, S. R. 1977. "Characteristics of Moral Dilemmas Written by Adolescents." *Developmental Psychology* 13:162–163.

Personal Communications

• Candee, D. June 19, 1981. P. 83

• Kohlberg, L. June 28, 1983. P. 21

• Kohlberg, L. June 28, 1983. P. 116

• Rau, W. January 21, 1985. P. 86

• Schrader, D. October 5, 1987. P. 19

INDEX